Restoring U.S. Leadership in Nuclear Energy

A National Security Imperative

THE CSIS COMMISSION ON NUCLEAR ENERGY
POLICY IN THE UNITED STATES

A Report of the CSIS Nuclear Energy Program

June 2013

50 YEARS | CHARTING OUR FUTURE

CSIS | CENTER FOR STRATEGIC & INTERNATIONAL STUDIES

ROWMAN & LITTLEFIELD
Lanham • Boulder • New York • Toronto • Plymouth, UK

About CSIS—50th Anniversary Year

For 50 years, the Center for Strategic and International Studies (CSIS) has developed solutions to the world's greatest policy challenges. As we celebrate this milestone, CSIS scholars are developing strategic insights and bipartisan policy solutions to help decisionmakers chart a course toward a better world.

CSIS is a nonprofit organization headquartered in Washington, D.C. The Center's 220 full-time staff and large network of affiliated scholars conduct research and analysis and develop policy initiatives that look into the future and anticipate change.

Founded at the height of the Cold War by David M. Abshire and Admiral Arleigh Burke, CSIS was dedicated to finding ways to sustain American prominence and prosperity as a force for good in the world. Since 1962, CSIS has become one of the world's preeminent international institutions focused on defense and security; regional stability; and transnational challenges ranging from energy and climate to global health and economic integration.

Former U.S. senator Sam Nunn has chaired the CSIS Board of Trustees since 1999. Former deputy secretary of defense John J. Hamre became the Center's president and chief executive officer in April 2000.

CSIS does not take specific policy positions; accordingly, all views expressed herein should be understood to be solely those of the author(s).

The views expressed in this document should be understood to be solely those of the authors. The conclusions herein do not necessarily reflect the positions of individual commission members or any affiliated organizations.

x

© 2013 by the Center for Strategic and International Studies. All rights reserved.

Library of Congress Cataloging-in-Publication Data
CIP information available on request.

ISBN: 978-1-4422-2511-4 (pb); 978-1-4422-2512-1 (eBook)

Center for Strategic and International Studies
1800 K Street, NW, Washington, DC 20006
202-887-0200 | www.csis.org

Rowman & Littlefield Publishers, Inc.
4501 Forbes Boulevard, Lanham, MD 20706
301-459-3366 | www.rowman.com

Contents

ABOUT THE CSIS NUCLEAR ENERGY PROGRAM

The Nuclear Energy Program at CSIS collaborates with industry, government, and the non-governmental sector to address the challenges facing the peaceful use of nuclear energy, including the challenges to the existing U.S. fleet. The case for U.S. leadership in nuclear energy, domestically and globally, is based on various dimensions of national security benefits to the U.S. While there are several critical areas of focus going forward, a principal area of immediate focus in the program will be the development and deployment of Small Modular Reactors (SMRs).

The United States may face a substantial contraction of commercial nuclear energy in the coming years. Very low prices for natural gas have fundamentally transformed the energy economy, with many positive benefits, but in so doing also contributed to a reduction in the competitiveness of commercial nuclear power. In addition, state and federal mandates and direct and indirect subsidies for renewable energy—particularly wind—create market distortions in the electricity sector that contribute to undermining the economic viability of nuclear power. Together, these forces are causing nuclear energy facilities to become increasingly uneconomic, particularly in competitive state electricity markets. Indeed, as many as a quarter of commercial nuclear energy facilities in America are cash-flow negative, or may be soon, or could be facing difficult investment decisions which may lead to early shutdowns.

Such a contraction would have a significant impact beyond the commercial nuclear energy sector, affecting university physics and engineering programs, materials, science laboratories, manufacturers, labor programs for training nuclear welders, and much more. It would undoubtedly affect the defense establishment and our nuclear Navy's capabilities, as well as the United States' ability to shape global standards for safety, security, operations, emergency response and nonproliferation.

Ongoing Work:

- Promote policies that ensure regulatory prioritization and increase regulatory certainty for the commercial nuclear energy sector.
- Educate policymakers on the market distortions created by certain targeted mandates and subsidies (direct and indirect) that put additional pressure on the economic viability of nuclear power, thus undermining U.S. national interests.
- Model the impact of a significant reduction in the number of operating nuclear power plants on the U.S. economy and defense establishment, including forecasting scenarios depicting a significant sectoral collapse. Conversely, model the impact of a healthy sectoral expansion.
- Advance the development and deployment of small modular reactors (SMRs) in a manner to support U.S. interests. Include consideration for deployment at military bases and government facilities, helping to insulate those facilities from cyber attack, while providing clean and reliable electricity.
- Encourage policies that result in the expansion of export markets for U.S. companies to help preserve domestic manufacturing capacity for nuclear technologies.

About the CSIS Commission on Nuclear Energy Policy in the United States

The CSIS Commission on Nuclear Energy in the United States is made up of senior public and private sector officials from across the political spectrum who agree that nuclear energy is an important part of this country's energy mix and that the United States is losing ground as other countries proceed with planned expansions of their nuclear sectors.

Concerns about the national security implications of a diminished U.S. presence in the global nuclear energy market are real. The Commission has provided insights on the benefits and challenges associated with nuclear energy, laying a foundation for public policy in this area. A variety of areas have been considered including environmental considerations, financial structuring, safety, regulatory structures, nonproliferation, trade, domestic economic impact, infrastructure contribution, national security, and waste.

Commission Structure and Events

- The Commission convened at CSIS on September 14th, 2011 to review the project's goals and agree on areas of work for a draft report.
- High-level subgroups made up of commissioners and outside advisors with expertise in a variety of areas provided input for critical work areas including financial structuring, implications of the Fukushima disaster, supply chain and labor concerns, opportunities for global collaboration, and national security implications.
- Throughout 2012, the CSIS U.S. Nuclear Energy Project staff engaged experts in various areas of industry and government to gain insight on the challenges facing nuclear energy and recommendations for next steps.
- The Commission's goals included providing recommendations that are substantive and actionable; this final report is intended to be a comprehensive, bipartisan, and credible treatment of this critical topic.

THE CSIS COMMISSION ON NUCLEAR ENERGY POLICY IN THE UNITED STATES

COCHAIRS

Lt. Gen. Brent Scowcroft
Trustee, CSIS

Mayo Shattuck
Chairman of the Board, Exelon

Michael Wallace
Senior Adviser, CSIS

COMMISSION MEMBERS

Mark Ayers*
President, Building & Construction Trades Department, AFLT-CIO

David Christian
CEO, Dominion Generation

J.D. Crouch
President, Technology Solutions Group, QinetiQ North America

Charles Curtis
President Emeritus & Board Member, Nuclear Threat Initiative

James Ellis
President & CEO, Institute of Nuclear Power Operations (retired)

William Fehrman
President & CEO, MidAmerican Energy Company

Marvin Fertel
President & CEO, Nuclear Energy Institute

Gary Gates
President & CEO, Omaha Public Power District

C. Boyden Gray
Founding Partner, Boyden Gray & Associates LLP

John Hamre
President, CEO, and Pritzker Chair, CSIS

Tom Kilgore
President & CEO, Tennessee Valley Authority (retired)

Dale Klein
Associate Director, Energy Institute, University of Texas at Austin

Richard Meserve
President, Carnegie Institution of Washington

Patrick Moore
Chairman & Chief Scientist, Greenspirit Strategies, Ltd.

James Rogers
Chairman, President & CEO, Duke Energy

James Schlesinger
Chairman, The MITRE Corporation

Clay Sell
President, Hunt Energy Horizons

* Commissioner Ayers served until his untimely death in April 2012. He was a great friend and adviser and we dedicate this report to his memory.

REPORT AUTHORS

Michael Wallace
John Kotek
Sarah Williams
Paul Nadeau
Thomas Hundertmark
George David Banks

EXECUTIVE SUMMARY

RESTORING U.S. LEADERSHIP IN NUCLEAR ENERGY:
A NATIONAL SECURITY IMPERATIVE

America's nuclear energy industry is in decline. Low natural gas prices, financing hurdles, failure to find a permanent repository for high-level nuclear waste, reactions to the Fukushima accident in Japan, and other factors are hastening the day when existing U.S. reactors become uneconomic, while making it increasingly difficult to build new ones. Two generations after the United States took this wholly new and highly sophisticated technology from laboratory experiment to successful commercialization, our nation is in danger of losing an industry of unique strategic importance and unique promise for addressing the environmental and energy security demands of the future.

The decline of the U.S. nuclear energy industry could be much more rapid than policymakers and stakeholders anticipate. With 102 operating reactors and the world's largest base of installed nuclear capacity, it has been widely assumed that the United States—even without building many new plants—would continue to have a large presence in this industry for decades to come. Instead, current market conditions are such that growing numbers of units face unprecedented financial pressures and could be retired early. Early retirements, coupled with scheduled license expirations and dim prospects for new construction, point to diminishing domestic opportunities for U.S. nuclear energy firms.

The outlook is much different in China, India, Russia, and other countries, where governments are looking to significantly expand their nuclear energy commitments. Dozens of new entrants plan

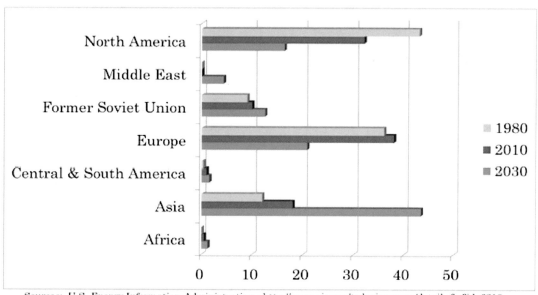

Regional Shares of Installed Global Nuclear Generating Capacity

Sources: U.S. Energy Information Administration - http://www.eia.gov/todayinenergy/detail.cfm?id=6310 (historical data); McKinsey & Co (2030 forecast)

on adding nuclear technology to their generating mix, furthering the spread of nuclear materials and know-how around the globe. It is in our nation's best interest that U.S. companies meet a significant share of this demand for nuclear technology—not simply because of trade and employment benefits, but because exports of U.S.-origin technology and materials are accompanied by conditions that protect our nonproliferation interests. Yet U.S. firms are currently at a competitive disadvantage in global markets due to restrictive and otherwise unsupportive export policies. U.S. efforts to facilitate peaceful uses of nuclear technology helped build a global nuclear energy infrastructure—but that infrastructure could soon be dominated by countries with less proven nonproliferation records. Without a strong commercial presence in new nuclear markets, America's ability to influence nonproliferation policies and nuclear safety behaviors worldwide is bound to diminish.

In this context, federal action to reverse the U.S. nuclear industry's impending decline is a national security imperative. The United States cannot afford to become irrelevant in a new nuclear age. This brief outlines why.

MAKING THE CONNECTION: HOW A STRONG CIVIL NUCLEAR INDUSTRY SUPPORTS U.S. NATIONAL SECURITY OBJECTIVES

From the start of the nuclear era until the 1980s, the United States was the dominant global supplier of commercial nuclear energy technology. American leadership was instrumental in shaping the global nuclear nonproliferation regime and nuclear safety norms. A strong domestic nuclear program and supportive government policies helped sustain this dominant position. Today, the United States continues to exercise influence by virtue of its economic power and recognized expertise in facility operations, safety, and security. But our nation's ability to promote nonproliferation and other national security objectives through peaceful nuclear cooperation has diminished.

Projected Installed Global Nuclear Generating Capacity - 2030

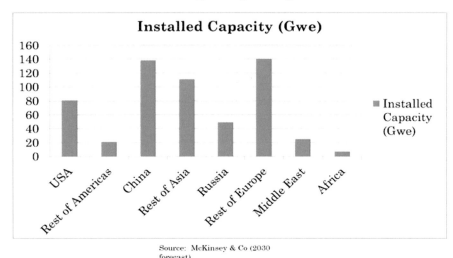

Source: McKinsey & Co (2030 forecast)

An important source of U.S. leverage in the past was the ability to provide reliable nuclear technologies, fuel, and services to countries under strict nonproliferation controls and conditions. These controls and conditions go beyond provisions in the Treaty on the Non-Proliferation of Nuclear Weapons and include nine criteria that the United States applies to any agreement with a nonnuclear weapon state: for example, a guarantee that the recipient state will not enrich or reprocess transferred nuclear material without U.S. approval.

Who is building the world's new nuclear reactors?
Reactors Planned and Under Construction by Home Country of Reactor Provider

India 4%
ROW* 6%
France 8%
Korea 10%
USA 7%
Russia 37%
China** 28%

*Rest of World: Canada, Germany, Japan
**39 Additional reactors are planned in China, but have not been assigned a technology provider.
(Currrent as of 5/7/2012)

Data from World Nuclear Association

Today, much of the world's nuclear manufacturing and supply capability still relies on designs and technologies developed in the United States. But the firms involved are largely foreign-owned. Even in the market for conventional light-water reactors, where the United States led the world for decades, all but one of the U.S.-based designers and manufacturers have been acquired by non-U.S.-based competitors.

The countries that are currently strengthening their nuclear capabilities and global market position (i.e., France, Japan, South Korea, and Russia, with China close behind) have different reasons for pursuing nuclear technology—some are primarily concerned about energy security or about preserving domestic fossil fuel resources, while others may be motivated by a mix of nationalistic and geopolitical considerations. But in all cases they see nuclear technology as offering long-term benefits that justify a significant near-term sovereign investment, even faced with the prospect that world natural gas prices may fall if the unconventional gas production technologies in use in the United States are successfully applied in other parts of the world.

The most aggressive of these new national nuclear programs is underway in China. By 2020, China could have 50 commercial reactors in operation, compared with only 3 in 2000. India could add 7 new plants—and Russia, 10—in the next five years. These trends are expected to accelerate out to 2030, by which time China, India, and Russia could account for nearly 40 percent of global nuclear generating capacity.

Meanwhile, many smaller nations—mostly in Asia and the Middle East—are planning to get into the nuclear energy business for the first time. In all, as many as 15 new nations could have nuclear generating capacity within the next two decades, added to the more than 30 countries that have it today or have had it in the past.

The national security concern is that much of this new interest in nuclear power is coming from countries and regions that may not share America's interests and priorities in the areas of nonproliferation and global security. And our leverage to influence their nuclear programs will be weak at best if U.S. companies cannot offer the technologies, services, and expertise these countries need to operate a successful nuclear program (including not only reactors, but other fuel-cycle facilities).

Expanded nuclear electricity generation outside the United States will drive a commensurate increase in the demand for enriched uranium. The facilities needed to supply this demand—

because they can be used to produce both nuclear fuel and nuclear weapons-usable material—are of particular national security concern.

During the 1960s, the U.S. operated the only uranium enrichment facility wholly dedicated to producing low-enriched uranium (LEU) for commercial purposes. Today, the single U.S.-based enrichment company, USEC, accounts for less than 20 percent of global LEU production capacity. USEC recently announced the shutdown of uranium enrichment at its only operating plant in Paducah, Kentucky, which was viewed as being outdated and too inefficient to be competitive with foreign suppliers.

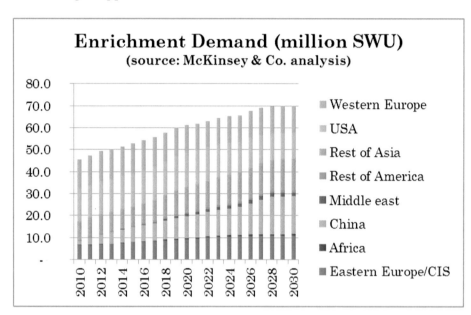

In fact, much of the fuel used in U.S. reactors today is fabricated from imported enriched uranium obtained by USEC under a very successful agreement with the Russian government to supply down-blended highly enriched uranium, a contract that expires in 2013. Although USEC plans to replace the aging Paducah plant with a more advanced facility, prospects for following through on this plan are far from certain. Meanwhile, the European uranium enrichment company (Urenco) is expanding its market share worldwide with several new facilities planned or under construction in Europe and the United States. In addition, Russia is taking steps to modernize its enrichment services capability. All told, the U.S. share of global exports for enriched uranium and other sensitive nuclear materials declined from approximately 29 percent in 1994 to 10 percent in 2008.

A healthy domestic nuclear infrastructure also serves our national security interests by supporting the nuclear propulsion program of the U.S. Navy, which operates a fleet of 83 nuclear-powered submarines and aircraft carriers. While the Navy is careful to develop sources of supply that can weather short-term ups and downs in the commercial industry, a sustained decline in the commercial industry could have a direct and negative impact on the naval program.

Finally, the U.S. nuclear industry contributes to energy security at home. Today, nuclear power plants supply nearly 20 percent of U.S. electricity needs while also playing a central role in assuring grid reliability in several regions of the county and avoiding significant air pollution and greenhouse gas emissions. Yet with uncertainty about the prospects for new plant construction over the next decade and with nearly all existing plants scheduled to be shut down by 2050, the share of electricity generated by nuclear reactors in the United States will decline steadily to near zero by mid-century. By that time, the United States could be host to as little as 2 percent of global installed nuclear capacity—down from 25 percent today.

Nuclear power has been an important part of the U.S. energy mix for decades. Today's economics, however, do not support the construction of new nuclear power plants, in the United States, where a recent significant drop in natural gas prices is radically altering the competitive outlook for different generation options. It is no coincidence that new nuclear commitments are being made in countries where the government is the primary investor. Unlike private investors, governments can take a longer view and can factor non-economic considerations into their energy choices. They have the ability and an obligation to act in support of the broader national interest.

In the United States, where energy resource decisions are left largely to the market, the challenge is to forge bipartisan political support for policies that help align private incentives with the national interest. This is particularly difficult at a time when extreme constraints on public spending and deep distrust of government intervention and large energy companies alike make a comprehensive energy strategy unlikely. But if a vibrant commercial nuclear industry is critical for U.S. long-term energy and national security, the federal government must act to address the drivers of the industry's decline. That means both ensuring that U.S. export policies enable U.S. companies to compete successfully in international markets and overcoming hurdles that threaten to preclude new nuclear investments in the United States for the foreseeable future.

EXPORT MARKET CHALLENGES

America's declining role in global export markets for nuclear technology represents a major lost opportunity in terms of jobs, technological leadership, and our nation's balance of trade. It is also a critical national security issue, for all the reasons discussed above. Reversing this decline requires a critical look at current U.S. export policies and at options for helping American companies compete more effectively with foreign suppliers.

A necessary first step is to adopt a consistent and flexible approach to negotiating the "123 Agreements" that currently govern transfers of reactors, reactor components, or special nuclear material, source material, and byproduct material under license for commercial, medical, and industrial purposes to overseas customers (the term refers to Section 123 of the Atomic Energy Act). The United States has Section 123 Agreements in place with 21 individual countries, the European Atomic Energy Community (EURATOM) consortium (which includes 27 countries), Taiwan, and the International Atomic Energy Agency (IAEA). Seven of these agreements are scheduled to expire by 2015 (including those with major trading partners such as China, South Korea, and Taiwan); in addition, the United States does not have agreements in place with several nations that are developing new nuclear programs, including Saudi Arabia and Vietnam. Despite the clear need to renew or establish agreements with nations that are investing in nuclear energy, some members of Congress have advocated for the inclusion of additional restrictions that will make it more difficult to execute such agreements. While the Obama administration earlier announced that 123 Agreements would be negotiated on a case-by-case basis and that no blanket provisions would be pursued in future agreements, most important is putting priority on timely reviews of such agreements. Given the different views of the administration and key congressional leaders, the already-slow 123 Agreement process may grind to a halt.

While debate continues on whether future 123 Agreements contain provisions to restrict the development of enrichment and reprocessing technology within a sovereign nation, approval of a

Section 123 Agreement only lays the foundation for U.S. trade in nuclear technology. Detailed export licensing requirements must still be satisfied, such as the 10 CFR Part 810 regulations that control the transfer of technology and other assistance to foreign nuclear energy programs. Recent administration proposals would make these requirements harder to satisfy. And even when agreements have been reached and export requirements have been satisfied, U.S. firms must compete with firms from other nations on the basis of technological competitiveness, cost, and other considerations. While U.S.-based firms still offer some of the most advanced technology available anywhere, they do not benefit, as many of their competitors do, from attractive, government-backed export incentives. Russian exporters—which currently account for more than one-third of the new reactors that are under construction or planned worldwide—at times offer turnkey services and fuel take-back programs, making deals with Russian firms attractive for countries with limited nuclear infrastructure. As a result of these and other factors, and in sharp contrast to our position of a few decades ago, the United States has become a net importer of nuclear components and materials.

Looking ahead to future markets, some 60 countries that do not currently have nuclear power plants have approached the IAEA to explore the possibility of acquiring one. The IAEA anticipates that about 15 of these aspiring nuclear nations will proceed to build one or more reactors over the next decade or two. In many of these nations (and in some nations that already have nuclear energy), a large nuclear plant may be poorly suited to local needs. Small modular reactors (SMRs) may offer a better fit for nations with smaller or slower-growing electrical demand. Cooperative public-private efforts are underway in the United States to explore the commercial potential of SMR technology, but the present pace of development may be insufficient to prevent other nations from capturing the lion's share of this potential new market.

DOMESTIC CHALLENGES

The challenges facing new nuclear plants in the United States come primarily in four areas: cost, waste management, regulation, and public acceptance.

High capital costs, together with long timeframes for licensing and construction and the increasing cost-competitiveness of alternative forms of generation, mean that new nuclear power plants are effectively out of the running compared to other generation options. Simply put, nuclear plants are large, long-term investments that often don't fit the needs of the small and diverse set of U.S. utilities that are focused primarily on meeting near-term business objectives. This is particularly true in markets in the United States and in some other nations where nuclear has to compete with low-cost gas and where utility-sector deregulation means no guarantee of cost recovery (see figure below; note that spot prices are roughly $4 per million BTU). Unfortunately, the incentives introduced under the Energy Policy Act of 2005—including loan guarantees and standby insurance—have met with limited success. While four new reactors are being built in Georgia and South Carolina—which is an important and positive development—the EPAct incentives have failed to produce more than a handful of new plant commitments in the United States. Future designs, such as small modular reactors, may reduce some of these competitive disadvantages, but a lack of field experience makes meaningful cost comparisons difficult at this time.

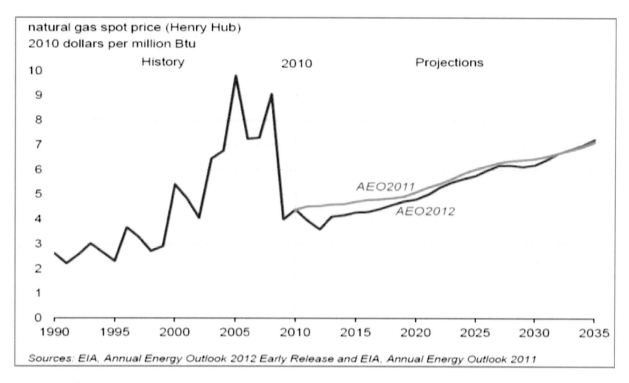

natural gas spot price (Henry Hub)
2010 dollars per million Btu

History   2010   Projections

AEO2011

AEO2012

Sources: EIA, Annual Energy Outlook 2012 Early Release and EIA, Annual Energy Outlook 2011

Access to financing is particularly challenging when the amount of capital required to build a new two-unit plant is upwards of $10 billion. Financing a civil nuclear facility, even with favorable economics, has long been a daunting undertaking for most private investors, particularly given the history of cost overruns with nuclear plant construction. New nuclear builds may therefore demand the involvement of large industrial companies, sovereign wealth, or other entities that have access to large amounts of capital and can take a long view of investment risks and returns.

Waste management has stood for decades as a barrier to the growth of nuclear energy in the United States. Several states have laws that ban construction of new nuclear plants until the waste issue is resolved. More broadly, the lack of a waste-disposal solution has damaged the credibility of, and undermined public confidence in, nuclear power as an energy source.

The recent report of the Blue Ribbon Commission on America's Nuclear Future found that "this nation's failure to come to grips with the nuclear waste issue has already proved damaging and costly and it will be more damaging and more costly the longer it continues: damaging to prospects for maintaining a potentially important energy supply option for the future, damaging to state–federal relations and public confidence in the federal government's competence, and damaging to America's standing in the world—not only as a source of nuclear technology and policy expertise but as a leader on global issues of nuclear safety, non-proliferation, and security."

If the United States can decide on a course of action to deal with its own spent fuel and other high-level nuclear waste, this could open the door to options such as fuel "take-away" arrangements between the United States and countries with small nuclear programs. Such agreements, which would allow a country to dispose of spent fuel in another country with established disposal capability rather than on its own soil, could have large safety and security benefits, especially if implemented in concert with nonproliferation goals. The United States has had a small but successful security initiative to repatriate spent foreign research reactor fuel for storage and disposal. If a similar program to accept spent fuel from foreign commercial reactors could be established, this would greatly expand the options available to the United States in advancing its nonproliferation interests, particularly as new, small, and inexperienced nuclear entrants consider their fuel cycle options. Of course, such a program would likely be politically acceptable only in the context of discernible progress toward implementing a permanent disposal solution for U.S. spent fuel.

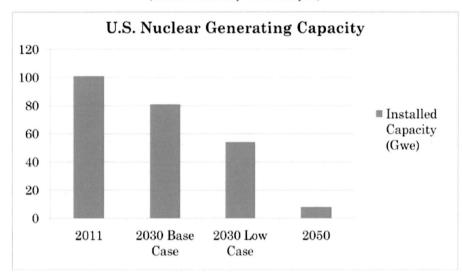

Increasing Financial Pressures Could Lead to Even More Rapid Reactor Shutdowns by 2030
(Source: McKinsey & Co. analysis)

The U.S. Nuclear Regulatory Commission (NRC) has set the global standard for excellence in nuclear energy regulation and has long served to bolster public confidence in nuclear operations. Yet there is a growing concern that the regulatory burden facing U.S. plant operators will be expanded without commensurate safety benefit, particularly in light of the understandable and appropriate desire to respond quickly to lessons learned from the Fukushima nuclear accident in Japan. It is essential that the NRC and the U.S. nuclear industry work constructively to enhance the safety and security of the U.S. nuclear fleet without placing undue burdens on reactor operators. The U.S. commercial industry has been unrelenting in its quest for excellence. The Institute of Nuclear Power Operations (INPO) has been a strong force for self-regulation and the result has been performance that sets the global standard. Added regulatory requirements when they produce real benefits are good for the industry; additional regulatory costs without appropriate benefits will weigh down otherwise well-performing nuclear facilities and their staff, and would contribute to financial pressures that could lead to even more rapid shutdowns of presently operating nuclear power plants.

Public acceptance of nuclear energy has fallen in the aftermath of the Fukushima accident. While most polls show a majority of Americans still support the use of nuclear energy, opposition to new plants in most parts of the country is still formidable. Sustained operational and regulatory excellence, competent and swift response to safety issues, and a path forward for the nuclear waste program can help turn the tide of public opinion.

RESTORING U.S. NUCLEAR LEADERSHIP—A TOOLKIT FOR POLICYMAKERS

Maintaining nuclear energy infrastructure at home and a leadership role in the nuclear arena abroad should be a national interest priority for the U.S. government. A robust domestic industry will deliver benefits for the American people beyond those recognized in the marketplace. It therefore warrants support beyond what the market—left to private considerations of risk and reward alone—will provide.

Of course, there is no single policy step the government can take to restore the strength of the U.S. nuclear industry. And government cannot do it all—industry will still need to develop attractive technology offerings and deliver a quality product or service consistent with the cost and schedule requirements of their customers. The goal of government support for the U.S. nuclear energy industry should be to improve the economic picture for nuclear at home and reduce barriers to participating in nuclear commerce abroad in order to increase the overall likelihood that the United States will have a strong domestic nuclear industry. In this section, we offer a range of policy actions that can move us toward this goal.

Many critical issues surrounding nuclear energy have come into sharp focus through the meetings, workshops, interviews, and research undertaken by the U.S. Nuclear Energy Project (USNEP) between March 2011 and June 2012. While our full report provides deeper background on those issues, this summary addresses them at a high level. In some cases, our recommendations echo those of other noteworthy reviews and reports; in other cases, they are a direct outgrowth of the work of USNEP.

BOLSTERING U.S. COMPETITIVENESS IN EXPORT MARKETS

Improving the ability of U.S. firms to compete in the global nuclear marketplace is the highest-priority recommendation of the Commission. Our reasoning is straightforward. A large-scale, government-supported nuclear construction program in the United States would be cost-prohibitive. On the other hand, there are several other nations that have placed a higher priority on the nonmonetary advantages of nuclear energy and are therefore aggressively investing in new reactors. Rather than rest our hopes primarily on an expensive program of domestic industry supports, we believe that recommendations focused on making it easier for U.S. firms to compete have a greater likelihood of being implemented and a greater chance of achieving our goals.

Specifically, we recommend adoption of the following policies:

- 123 Agreements: The negotiation of future 123 Agreements based on individual, unique bilateral relationships—rather than insisting that nations cede their NPT rights to nuclear fuel cycle technologies—is the approach most likely to support U.S. nuclear exports. This policy should be the norm and should be recognized as such by the U.S. Congress, with the understanding that U.S. exporters playing a role in the global nuclear technology trade facilitates continued U.S. leadership in global nuclear nonproliferation goals.
- Part 810 Requirements: Part 810 prohibits U.S. companies from assisting foreign nuclear power programs unless such assistance is authorized by the secretary of energy, following an interagency review process specified by the Atomic Energy Act. These requirements can stand in the way of U.S. nuclear companies' ability to conduct routine business. The current Part 810 rules are already restrictive, but changes proposed by Department of Energy (DOE) staff in 2011 would only make matters worse. We understand that a new revision of the Section 810 rules is being prepared; this version should take into full account the concerns raised by U.S. nuclear firms. Timely completion of reviews should be a priority.
- Government Support for Exports and Export Financing: Despite offering some of the best technology in the world, U.S. providers of nuclear technology find themselves at a

competitive disadvantage due in part to the lack of consistent and coordinated government support for nuclear exports. U.S.-based companies are competing against state-owned or -directed nuclear suppliers overseas that enjoy consistent government support for nuclear technology exports and can offer government-backed financing agreements that are far more attractive than those currently available to facilitate U.S. exports. Given that nuclear exports provide the Unites States with important leverage in nonproliferation, nuclear safety, and other matters, the federal government should issue a clear policy statement in support of nuclear technology exports, should ensure that this policy is implemented consistently by the relevant federal agencies, and should streamline the cumbersome export approval process.

EXPANDED SUPPORT FOR SMR TECHNOLOGY DEVELOPMENT

To regain a competitive edge in international nuclear markets, U.S. firms will need to offer technology that other nations want to buy. Given that the government benefits by having strong U.S. nuclear firms, it is appropriate for technology investments to be supported both by industry and by the federal government.

A specific area where the United States is active and has an opportunity to take a commercial lead is in developing and deploying small modular reactor (SMR) technology, which holds promise for reducing capital expenditure requirements and construction timelines. In particular, the U.S. government could accelerate the development of SMR technology using military and DOE facilities. In recent years, the U.S. Department of Defense (DOD) has become increasingly interested in the potential of SMRs for military applications. This interest stems mainly from two critical vulnerabilities that DOD has identified: the dependence of U.S. military bases on the domestic electrical grid, and the challenge of providing assured energy supply to troops in forward operating locations.

The U.S. government is already investing tens of millions of dollars per year in the development of SMR designs. This effort should be continued and expanded, as envisioned under DOE's current SMR program plans. Going forward, these plans should allow for the parallel development of materials, fabrication, manufacturing, assembly, and operation of SMRs by several different vendors. The idea would be to meet NRC licensing requirements while maintaining flexibility to innovate and iterate throughout the development process.

Following the successful development of SMR technology, vendors should be encouraged to pursue global market opportunities while also advancing the highest U.S. standards for safety, security, reliability, and emergency response as applicable to this new technology. The same economic and financial structuring incentives available for light-water reactors should also be made available for SMRs. Commercialization should be accompanied by adherence to traditional regulatory requirements and NRC oversight as a way to build public confidence in the commercial deployment of this technology.

Looking even longer-term, an aggressive government-industry nuclear research, development, and demonstration (RD&D) program can help form the basis for advanced (Generation IV) nuclear reactor and fuel cycle technologies that may be deployed around the middle of the century. This may seem like a long time horizon, but nuclear energy technologies now take decades to move through the R&D phases to demonstration and into commercial use; the Generation III+ reactor designs being built today in the United States, China, and other nations are based on technologies that entered development in the 1980s. The United States should continue to invest in similarly long-term R&D, including investments in the university and national laboratory research facility infrastructure needed to develop and demonstrate new nuclear technologies.

SOLVING THE NUCLEAR WASTE CHALLENGE

Demonstrating a credible path forward for nuclear waste management in the United States would both reduce public concerns about nuclear plant construction and satisfy laws in several states that prohibit new plant construction without a solution to the nuclear waste challenge. The dual challenges of spent nuclear fuel management and disposal are addressed at length in the final 2012 report of the Blue Ribbon Commission on America's Nuclear Future and the 2011 MIT Report on the Future of the Nuclear Fuel Cycle. We urge that the U.S. government act on recommendations in these reports as a critical step toward supporting the revival of the nuclear industry in the United States:

- Providing access to the funds nuclear utility ratepayers provide for the purpose of nuclear waste management.
- Establishing a new organization dedicated solely to implementing the waste management program and empowered with the authority and resources to succeed.
- Implementing a consent-based approach to siting future nuclear waste management facilities.
- Pursuing fuel-leasing options for countries that have or are pursuing small nuclear programs. These options should provide incentives to forego uranium enrichment and should incorporate spent-fuel take-back arrangements.
- Undertaking integrated system studies and experiments on innovative reactor and fuel cycle options, and selecting a limited set of options for more detailed analysis.

EXPANDED PARTICIPATION IN INTERNATIONAL NUCLEAR COOPERATION

The United States is widely respected internationally for its strong independent nuclear regulation and its successful industry self-governance model. The result has been demonstrated by top performance in safety, security, operations, and emergency response, which is recognized globally. The NRC is regularly engaged as the benchmark standard setter for regulators in other countries. The Institute of Nuclear Power Operations (INPO) is routinely approached for leadership and assistance in applying the same principles that govern U.S. industry nuclear operations to other operators around the globe. The World Association of Nuclear Operators (WANO), modeled after INPO, is evolving to influence safe operations globally. More recently, the International Framework for Nuclear Energy Cooperation (IFNEC) has evolved as an influential forum, with 62 participating nations, and a 5-nation steering committee (United States, United Kingdom, France, Japan, and China); it has been embraced by many countries expanding or seeking to enter the realm of nuclear operations as a key opportunity for gaining insight from the experiences of successful nuclear energy nations. IFNEC, in particular, with continued DOE leadership, is an opportune body for bringing forth and reinforcing the standards and principles for responsible and safe nuclear energy operations worldwide. Through these entities and others, the United States should broadly continue to leverage its regulatory and legal framework and its reputation for excellence in all aspects of nuclear energy development and operations to other nations, and especially to emerging nations seeking to establish nuclear energy as a new domestic source of electricity.

ECONOMIC SUPPORT AND FINANCIAL STRUCTURING FOR NEW U.S. REACTORS

A limited set of "first mover" financial incentives at both the federal and state levels can help jump-start the construction of new nuclear power plants in the United States. Below we present a wide array of options and opportunities for encouraging and facilitating investment in new construction. We recognize that the approaches presented below would all be costly and would be quite challenging to enact in this time of tight government budgets. We offer a range of options not with the expectation that all of them will be adopted, but with the conviction that implementing any of these options—at the federal level, within individual states, or both—will improve prospects for building several more new plants in the United States and thus help strengthen the U.S. nuclear industry.

FINANCING

We recommend action in two areas:

- *Loan Guarantees*
  The Loan Guarantee Program established by the Energy Policy Act of 2005 has been implemented in a manner that is inconsistent with the intent of the program and has not proved successful in spurring investment in new nuclear construction in the United States. It should be reviewed and revised in order to provide support for new light-water reactor (LWR) construction and SMR development.

- *Foreign Ownership*
  Encouraging broad opportunities for foreign ownership in new nuclear construction would ease the investment burden on relatively small market cap firms in the United States. Facilitating this will require changes to relevant codes and regulations so sovereign wealth funds, foreign investors, non-U.S.-owned companies, and pension funds are free to invest in U.S. nuclear plants. Foreign ownership should be allowed up to 90 percent of the equity value of the facility, contingent on a U.S.-based owner/operator recognized by the NRC retaining controlling interest. All matters related to the safety, security, and reliability of the facility, including the unalterable right to make capital calls on the owners of the facility in support of the safety, security, and reliability needs of the facility would remain with the U.S. owner/operator.

REVISIONS TO THE TAX CODE

The federal tax code provides mechanisms for the federal government to incent activity that is in the national interest and that the marketplace would not otherwise undertake. The Energy Policy Act of 2005 moved in this direction. Given the experience of the last several years, and the increased gap in the economic viability of new nuclear facilities, further expansion of these mechanisms would be beneficial in the following areas.

- Accelerated Depreciation (also known as "Bonus Depreciation") changes to relevant tax codes are needed to provide for depreciation at the time that investments are made. This kind of incentive provides benefits during the construction period, effectively offsetting the capital requirements for a new plant as it is being constructed.

- Tax Credits—changes to relevant tax codes to provide for a 30 percent investment tax credit upon project completion.[1]
- Property Tax Abatement—encourage state and local authorities to support an approach that excludes new facilities from property taxes for the first 10 years of operation, with a phase in of low tax requirements for the subsequent 5 years.

Monetization of external benefits

Mechanisms to provide monetary recognition of the societal benefits (such as low emissions and electricity supply diversification) of certain forms of energy supply would improve the prospects for new nuclear builds. Such mechanisms would have the effect of increasing the cost-competitiveness of nuclear-generated electricity. Given uncertainty regarding legislation to regulate carbon emissions, a more realistic means of monetizing the external benefits of nuclear-generated electricity may be through power purchase agreements with the U.S. government, including military bases.

INTERNAL GOVERNMENT POLICY COORDINATION

Successful implementation of these recommendations could be better assured if backed by senior-level policy coordination within government. Such coordination could take many forms, and we don't presume to know what arrangements will work best within a given administration or congressional body. Options include but are not limited to:

- A White House directed activity, providing interagency coordination and informed by the Quadrennial Energy Review process underway within DOE;
- A Cabinet member assigned responsibility for interagency coordination; and/or
- Congressional oversight of federal activities, either through a specific mandate to an existing committee(s) or through the establishment of a new oversight entity.

Consideration should also be given to forming a private-sector stakeholder advisory committee with representation from nuclear plant owners and operators, investors, labor groups, nuclear vendors and contractors, the financial sector, state officials, environmental advocates, and other organizations. This group would provide critical expertise and insight from outside the federal government in support of the common goal to maintain nuclear energy as a key component of electricity generation in the United States.

---

[1] As provided under 26 USC 45; see Database of State Incentives for Renewables and Efficiencies (DESIRE), "Renewable Electricity Production Tax Credit (PTC)," April 2013, http://dsireusa.org/incentives/incentive.cfm?Incentive_Code=US13F.

Chapter 1

NUCLEAR ENERGY IN THE UNITED STATES AND WORLDWIDE: CURRENT STATUS AND OUTLOOK

Nuclear power has been used to produce electricity since the early 1950s. Today there are more than 430 nuclear power reactors, with a total capacity of about 372 gigawatts electric (GWe), operating in 30 countries plus Taiwan.[1] An additional 70 units, totaling more than 60 GWe, are under construction.[2] During 2011, nuclear power produced more than 2.5 trillion kilowatt-hours (kWh) of electricity. Globally, the nuclear energy industry now has about 15,000 reactor-years of operating experience.[3]

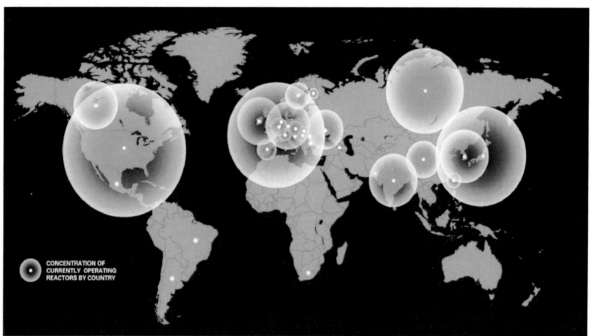

CONCENTRATION OF
CURRENTLY OPERATING
REACTORS BY COUNTRY

The contribution of nuclear energy to total electricity generation varies considerably from country to country and in different parts of the world. In Western Europe, nuclear-generated electricity accounts for almost 27 percent of total electricity supply. In both North America and Eastern Europe, it is approximately 18 percent. In the Far East, nuclear energy accounts for 10 percent of electricity generation, whereas in Africa and Latin America it is 2.1 percent and 2.4 percent, respectively. In the Middle East and South Asia, it accounts for just 1 percent.[4]

As shown above, nuclear energy use is concentrated in technologically advanced countries. Over the past two years the overall contribution of nuclear generation to world electricity production has declined slightly, from 15 percent to less than 14 percent.[5] This decline is largely due to an

---

[1] International Atomic Energy Agency (IAEA), Power Reactor Information System (PRIS), "The Database on Nuclear Power Reactors," http://www.iaea.org/PRIS/home.aspx.
[2] Ibid.
[3] Ibid, p. 4.
[4] Ibid.
[5] "Global Commercial Nuclear Power Capacity Outlook for 2030," McKinsey & Company, February 2012.

increase in total electricity generation worldwide without a commensurate increase in the nuclear contribution.[6]

A number of countries with existing nuclear power programs have significantly expanded investment in future nuclear power plants. From 2008 to 2012, there were 49 construction starts around the world, extending a growth trend that started in 2003 (however, in 2011, the number of new starts fell to 2).[7] Notably, in 2008 and 2009, all of the 22 construction starts were pressurized water reactors (PWRs) in three countries: China, the Republic of Korea, and Russia.[8]

The United States currently has 102 commercial reactors in operation with a total generating capacity of 101 GWe. These reactors produce about 19 percent of U.S. electricity. Four new units (two at the Vogtle site in Georgia and two at the V. C. Summer site in South Carolina) are under construction. Construction of one partially completed reactor (at the Tennessee Valley Authority's Watts Bar site) resumed in 2007 with a target completion date of December 2015. Planning for about two dozen other new reactors has been underway; these plants are in various stages of the licensing process but none is expected to be in operation prior to 2020.

U.S. Commercial Nuclear Power Reactors—
Years of Operation by the End of 2010

Years of Commercial Operation	Number of Reactors
△ 0–9	0
▲ 10–19	3
▲ 20–29	48
▲ 30–39	46
▲ 40 plus	7

Note: Ages have been rounded up to the end of the year.

Source: U.S. Nuclear Regulatory Commission

---

[6] Ibid., p. 5.
[7] Fiona Harvey et al., "Dramatic fall in new nuclear power stations after Fukushima," *The Guardian*, March 8, 2012, http://www.guardian.co.uk/environment/2012/mar/08/fall-nuclear-power-stations-fukushima.
[8] IAEA, Power Reactor Information System, http://www.iaea.org/PRIS/home.aspx.

The U.S. military is also a major user of nuclear-generated energy: about 40 percent of the major combat vessels in the U.S. Navy are nuclear powered. The Navy operates a fleet of 83 nuclear-powered submarines and aircraft carriers, which together employ a total of 103 nuclear reactors (aircraft carriers have at least 2 and as many as 8 reactors per vessel).[9] In 2008, the Navy began work on the Gerald R. Ford class of nuclear-powered aircraft carriers—the first of these carriers is slated to be delivered in 2015 and will replace the USS Enterprise (pictured at right), which was deployed in 1961.[10]

THE OUTLOOK FOR COMMERCIAL NUCLEAR ENERGY IN THE UNITED STATES

The outlook for commercial nuclear energy in the United States and abroad has changed considerably over just the past five years. This section provides a brief overview of some of the reasons for this change; a more detailed discussion of the specific challenges that nuclear energy confronts in the United States can be found in Chapter 3 of this report.

In terms of the domestic market for nuclear energy, by far the most important recent development has been a sharp decline in natural gas prices.[11] As a result, the cost of gas-fired electricity—which is driven largely by natural gas price—has fallen by nearly half over the past four years.[12] This drop in price has contributed to a large increase in the amount of U.S. electricity generated from natural gas, from 18.5 percent in 2003, to 21.6 percent in 2007, and to 30 percent in 2012.[13]

At the same time, increased safety and security requirements have considerably increased fixed operating costs for existing nuclear power plants.[14] This trend is expected to continue as new requirements are being imposed in the aftermath of the Fukushima-Daiichi accident in Japan.[15]

---

[9] U.S. Department of Energy, "FY 2013 Congressional Budget Request," Volume 1, p. 482, http://energy.gov/sites/prod/files/FY13Volume1.pdf.
[10] See naval-technology.com, "Gerald R. Ford Class (CVN 78/79)—U.S. Navy CVN 21 Future Carrier Programme, United States of America," http://www.naval-technology.com/projects/cvn-21/.
[11] U.S. Energy Information Agency, Natural Gas, http://www.eia.gov/dnav/ng/hist/n9190us3a.htm.
[12] See electricity production cost data at Nuclear Energy Institute, http://www.nei.org/resourcesandstats/documentlibrary/reliableandaffordableenergy/graphicsandcharts/uselectricityproductioncostsandcomponents/.
[13] U.S. Energy Information Administration, Electric Power Monthly, Data for February 2013, see http://www.eia.gov/electricity/monthly/epm_table_grapher.cfm?t=epmt_1_1.
[14] MIT, "The Future of the Nuclear Fuel Cycle," 2011, http://mitei.mit.edu/system/files/The_Nuclear_Fuel_Cycle-all.pdf.
[15] Nuclear Regulatory Commission, "Implementing Lessons Learned from Fukushima," http://www.nrc.gov/reactors/operating/ops-experience/japan-info.html.

THE FUTURE OF CHEAP GAS?

Many analysts predict continued upward movement in gas prices over the next several years. Why? The number of rigs drilling for natural gas in the United States has collapsed in the last 12 to 18 months – from about 900 rigs at work in late 2011 to about 400 today. Experts believe that sustaining current natural gas production takes about 600 rigs, so production may start to drift down with gas prices testing $5 per million BTU in 2014 and 2015. This is part of the normal cyclicality associated with a commodity business.

In addition, the United States may be seriously underestimating the prodigious volumes of natural gas consumed by a gas-fired combined-cycle plant running at full load. A one-thousand-megawatt gas plant burns more gas in a day than daily peak sendout for Boston Gas or Washington Natural Gas in Seattle. A 1,000-megawatt gas plant running at 90 percent capacity factor burns about 60 billion cubic feet a year—slightly less than New Hampshire's entire natural gas consumption in 2011 and more gas than 22 states burned for electric power production in 2011.

This combination of factors means that the economic viability of some smaller nuclear power plants in competitive electricity markets is in serious doubt. If electricity prices remain low and regulatory burdens continue to rise, it is quite possible that the operators of these reactors will decide to shut them down early rather than invest in major equipment change-outs or in the other capital-intensive plant upgrades and maintenance that will be required to operate the reactors to the end of their licensed operating lives. In May 2013, for example, Dominion retired its 556-megawatt Kewaunee nuclear power station approximately 20 years before the expiration of its license. Located outside of Green Bay, Kewaunee is the first early retirement of a nuclear plant explicitly due to competition from abundant, cheap natural gas and Powder River Basin coal, as well as large volumes of government-backed wind power. Kewaunee is the second plant to be shut down for economic reasons in 2013; in February, it was announced that the Crystal River nuclear plant was being retired when it was determined that repairs to the containment could not be made economically.

Low gas prices, increased public apprehension, and additional NRC requirements resulting from the Fukushima nuclear accident in Japan have had an even more dampening effect on prospects for building new plants in the United States. This is particularly true in competitive electricity markets, but it is also the case in regulated ones. Meanwhile, a federal loan guarantee program that was expected to help reduce nuclear power plant financing costs has thus far been met with limited success.

2012 U.S. Electricity Generation by Energy Source

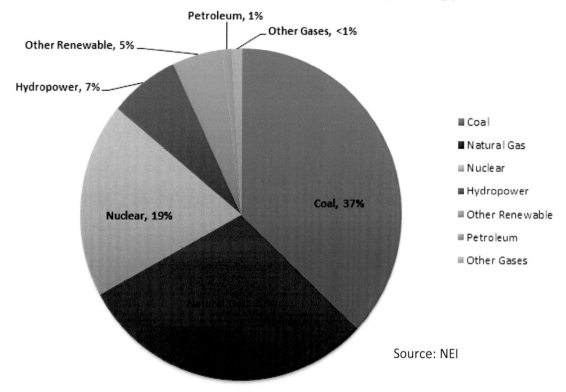

Petroleum, 1%

Other Gases, <1%

Other Renewable, 5%

Hydropower, 7%

Nuclear, 19%

Coal, 37%

Natural Gas, 30%

- Coal
- Natural Gas
- Nuclear
- Hydropower
- Other Renewable
- Petroleum
- Other Gases

Source: NEI

The economics for new plants in the United States are sufficiently challenging that it has proven quite difficult for some regulated owner/operators to take on the liabilities of seeing a new plant through the construction phase. While several state public utility commissions have provided or may provide the kind of rate treatment that can allow nuclear construction to proceed—as regulators are currently doing in Georgia, South Carolina, and a few other states—they are aware

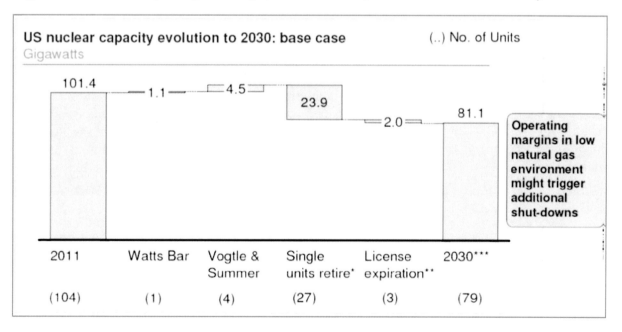

US nuclear capacity evolution to 2030: base case   (..) No. of Units

Gigawatts

101.4   — 1.1 —   ⌐ 4.5 ⌐   23.9   ═ 2.0 ═   81.1

Operating margins in low natural gas environment might trigger additional shut-downs

2011	Watts Bar	Vogtle & Summer	Single units retire*	License expiration**	2030***
(104)	(1)	(4)	(27)	(3)	(79)

that by doing so they are shifting risks and liabilities to the ratepayer.[16] Governors and legislatures, even in some states that are currently supportive of nuclear energy, may not be able to sustain that support, particularly if new plants experience the types of cost overruns and schedule delays that plagued reactors built in the United States in the 1970s and 1980s. Georgia Power has already announced a schedule delay at Vogtle due to delays in obtaining necessary regulatory approvals from the Nuclear Regulatory Commission.

If no new plants follow the Vogtle and Summer units, the picture for U.S. nuclear power production in 2030 could be very different than current government projections indicate. According to the reference case forecast by the U.S. Energy Information Administration, the United States will have about 110 GWe of nuclear generating capacity in 2030. By contrast, we project that nuclear capacity could drop to about 81 GWe by that date and to near zero by 2050.

THE OUTLOOK FOR COMMERCIAL NUCLEAR ENERGY OUTSIDE THE UNITED STATES

Looking abroad, a major shift also appears imminent in the global outlook for nuclear power. Until recently, Japan had the third-largest civil nuclear fleet—with nuclear power accounting for nearly 30 percent of overall generating capacity. The country's nuclear power program, however, suffered a major setback with the Fukushima accident, which resulted in a decision to shut down all nuclear plants in the country. Two reactors were later restarted as an emergency measure to avoid power shortages, but it remains an open question whether the remaining reactors will ever be restarted. Even with a return to service, 12 existing reactors will cease operation by 2020, absent life extensions, followed by an additional 18 reactors by 2030. Moreover, Prime Minister Shinzo Abe's pledge to restart reactors that meet strict new safety guidelines has been met with substantial resistance from local authorities and the public, which has lost confidence in the industry.

Certainly, the prospect for new builds in Japan is in serious doubt. Prior to the accident, Tokyo had planned to increase the nuclear contribution of overall power generation to 50 percent by 2030. Nine new nuclear reactors were to be brought on line by 2020 and five additional reactors by 2030. Already, the two reactors that were under construction at the time of the earthquake have been scrapped, and plans for other new plants have been put on hold.

In Western Europe, Germany, Belgium, Spain, and Switzerland have all decided to phase nuclear power out of their respective national energy portfolios over the next couple of decades. Italy, which had contemplated the introduction of commercial nuclear power plants, has since decided against it. However, other European nations—including Finland, Poland, the Czech Republic, and the United Kingdom—continue to press forward with new nuclear power development. France, which has the world's second-largest fleet of reactors, remains the region's staunchest supporter, though President François Hollande campaigned in favor of reducing France's dependence on nuclear power from 75 to 50 percent by 2025. Nonetheless, despite plans to shut down the

---

[16] Sony Ben-Moshe et al., "Financing the Nuclear Renaissance: The Benefits and Potential Pitfalls of Federal & State Government Subsidies and the Future of Nuclear Power in California," *Energy Law Journal*, Vol. 30:497, 2009, p. 497.

country's oldest reactor at Fessenheim within five years, Hollande's government remains committed to completing the new reactor at Flamanville.[17]

Outside Western Europe and Japan, interest in expanding nuclear capacity as a way to help meet growing electricity demand persists despite the accident. Thus, other nations—particularly China, India, Russia, and South Korea—are expected to continue pursuing robust nuclear expansion plans. New nuclear energy projects also remain on the table for policymakers in Vietnam, Turkey, Lithuania, and Jordan, to name a few.

The next several subsections provide further details on the nuclear development plans of China, India, Russia, and South Korea, since these nations are expected to become the industry's most important growth markets for the next few decades. We return to the policy implications of this global shift in nuclear investment and influence later in this chapter.

Japan, Germany, Switzerland and Italy have taken drastic steps after the Fukushima accident

		Pre Fukushima	Post Fukushima
Shut down	Japan	12 reactors with ~10 GW capacity were shutdown for periodic inspection	• 2 reactors shutdown at govt.'s request (3GWe) • 6 reactors in cold shutdown (6GWe) • 4 reactors shutdown to be decommissioned (3GWe)
	Germany	1 reactor in long term shutdown for upgrades	• Immediate shut down of 8 reactors • Phase out by 2022 instead of 2030 for remaining 9 reactors
	Switzerland	N/A	• Complete phase out by 2034 without replacement[1]
	Italy	All reactors were shut down by 1990	• N/A
New build plans	Japan	14 planned/proposed reactors	• Cancellation of 14 planned/proposed reactors • 2 reactors under construction
	Germany	No plan for nuclear new build	• No plan for nuclear new build
	Switzerland	Add 2 new reactors of 1.6 GWe	• Plan dropped
	Italy	Referendum set on Jun 2011 for new nuclear plants	• No new build for at least 5 years[2] and likely much longer

1 Based on 50-year operating lifetimes, nuclear power generation in the country would cease in 2034
2 Length of time for which a referendum result is binding in the country

SOURCE: WNA, IAEA, Team Analysis

Working Draft - Last Modified 19/02/2013 16:09:43   Printed 2/24/2012 4:57:22 PM

---

[17] Tara Patel, "EDF Wins Reprieve as Hollande Cools on Greens Nuclear Pact," Bloomberg, April 25, 2012, http://www.bloomberg.com/news/2012-04-25/edf-wins-reprieve-as-hollande-cools-on-greens-nuclear-pact-1-.html.

THE FUKUSHIMA DAI-ICHI NUCLEAR ACCIDENT

The severe accident that occurred at Japan's Fukushima Dai-ichi nuclear power station in March 2011 prompted widespread concern about the safety of nuclear energy and cast serious doubts over prospects for expanding the role of nuclear energy in Japan and elsewhere.

On March 11, 2011, an earthquake measuring 9.0 on the Richter scale occurred 112 miles off the eastern coast of Japan. The earthquake was the third largest ever recorded worldwide. In the immediate aftermath of the quake, all three of the operating units at Fukushima Dai-ichi automatically shut down via seismic reactor protection system trips. While the earthquake caused a loss of all external power to the site, the emergency diesel generator automatically started as designed, and provided AC power to emergency systems.

Within an hour after the earthquake, however, a series of tsunamis—including one with an estimated height of 46 to 49 feet—arrived at the site. This tsunami exceeded the design basis tsunami height of 18.7 feet, and rendered many of the emergency diesel generators inoperable.

The loss of emergency power to run cooling systems in turn led to a build-up of decay heat in the three loaded reactors and in the spent fuel being held in storage pools on site. Additionally, hydrogen generated from the damaged fuel accumulated in the reactor buildings and resulted in explosions in Units 1, 3, and 4. As a result, both primary and secondary containment structures for the reactors were damaged and radioactive material was released. About a month after the earthquake, the Fukushima accident was given the highest rating for seriousness on the International Nuclear and Radiological Event scale—it was rated 7 on a scale that runs from 1 ("anomaly") to 7 (major accident).

In July 2012, two separate reports on the Fukushima disaster by the Japanese parliament and by a government-formed panel of investigators strongly faulted both the plant's operator, Tokyo Electric Power Company, and Japan's nuclear regulatory agency for failing to ensure that proper safeguards and emergency preparations were in place before the tsunami occurred, and for an inadequate response as the crisis unfolded. The government created a new regulatory body, the Nuclear Regulation Agency (NRA), under the Ministry of the Environment in September 2012. The agency is reviewing current regulations and adding new safety measures in the hopes of increasing public confidence in the industry. The new safety rules are scheduled to be completed by the end of summer 2013. The Japanese people elected a cautiously pro-nuclear government in December 2012. The current prime minister, Shinzo Abe, will seek to restart the nation's reactors after new NRA safety criteria are established and met by the operators.

China dwarfs the US regarding installed capacity in 2030

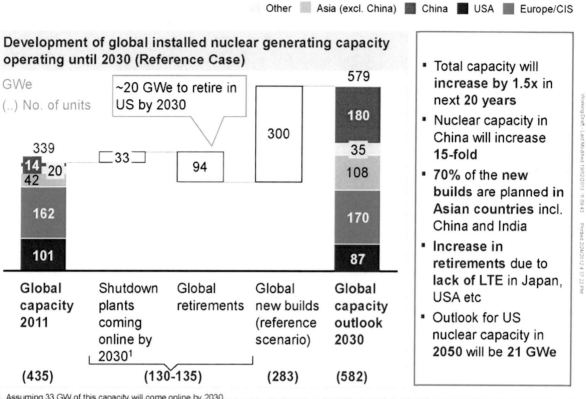

Other ▨ Asia (excl. China) ■ China ■ USA ■ Europe/CIS

Development of global installed nuclear generating capacity operating until 2030 (Reference Case)

GWe
(..) No. of units

~20 GWe to retire in US by 2030

579
180
35
108
170
87

339
14 20
42
162
101

33

94

300

Global capacity 2011

Shutdown plants coming online by 2030[1]

Global retirements

Global new builds (reference scenario)

Global capacity outlook 2030

(435)

(130-135)

(283)

(582)

- Total capacity will increase by 1.5x in next 20 years
- Nuclear capacity in China will increase 15-fold
- 70% of the new builds are planned in Asian countries incl. China and India
- Increase in retirements due to lack of LTE in Japan, USA etc
- Outlook for US nuclear capacity in 2050 will be 21 GWe

1. Assuming 33 GW of this capacity will come online by 2030

SOURCE: McKinsey nuclear model Q4 2011

CHINA

China—with current capacity only standing at about 13 GWe—is blazing ahead with the world's most aggressive civil nuclear expansion. With 17 reactors currently in operation, 28 units are being built, including 4 U.S.-designed AP1000 reactors at Sanmen and Haiyang. In response to Fukushima, Beijing postponed new approvals until reviews were held on the safety of existing plants and those under construction. By the summer of 2012, new safety standards for all nuclear facilities had been approved, giving the green light to plans to add more than 70 GWe of new capacity by the end of this decade.

The reactors that have been or are now being built rely on technology developed in many nations, including the United States, Russia, France, Japan, Canada, and others. A common theme across the wide variety of construction contracts signed by Chinese electricity providers has been the inclusion of aggressive requirements related to technology transfer. For example, Westinghouse has agreed to transfer technology to China's State Nuclear Power Technology Corporation (SNPTC) over the first four AP1000 units so that SNPTC can build subsequent units of this type on its own. In this way, China intends to transition from its current status as a nuclear technology importer to that of nuclear technology exporter over the next two decades.

Our analysis projects that China's demand for uranium and uranium enrichment services will grow nearly tenfold by 2030 (see figure below). Consequently, Beijing is pursuing an ambitious plan to lock up foreign uranium supplies—as it has done with other strategic minerals and resources. China will also increase its own production of uranium in Inner Mongolia and Xinjiang.

INDIA

India has an expanding and—until recently—largely indigenous nuclear power program, operating 20 nuclear reactors, which represent 4.4 GWe of generation capacity and supply about 4 percent of India's electricity.[18] India is building another seven reactors that will more than double its nuclear-electric production capacity.[19] It currently expects to have 20,000 MWe of nuclear capacity on line by 2020 and 63,000 MWe by 2032. India aims to supply 25 percent of its electricity from nuclear power by 2050.[20]

Because India is not a signatory to the Nuclear Non-Proliferation Treaty, it was largely excluded from global commercial nuclear markets over the past several decades until 2008. This hindered its development of civil nuclear energy, and as a result, India has for the most part developed its nuclear program without reactor fuel or technical assistance from other countries. Partly in response to its isolation from outside technical assistance and nuclear material supply, India has made independence in the nuclear fuel cycle and use of its abundant thorium reserves a major priority.[21]

Technical difficulties resulting from the isolation of its nuclear program contributed to India's power reactors having some of the world's lowest capacity factors up until the mid-1990s. But

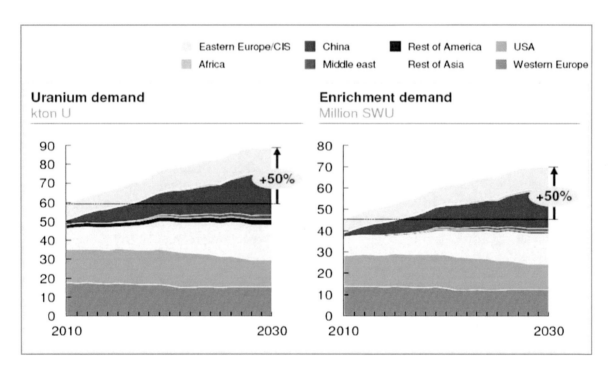

Source: McKinsey & Co. Analysis

---

[18] World Nuclear Association, "Nuclear Power in India," April 2013, http://www.world-nuclear.org/info/inf53.html.
[19] International Atomic Energy Agency, Power Reactor Information System, http://www.iaea.org/PRIS/home.aspx.
[20] Ibid.
[21] Ibid.

capacity factors rose to 60 percent in 1995 and 85 percent in 2001–2002. More recently, from 2008 to 2010, capacity factors dropped again due to a shortage of nuclear fuel.[22]

In September 2008, an agreement with the Nuclear Suppliers' Group—and a follow-on 2009 safeguards agreement with the International Atomic Energy Agency (IAEA)[23]—liberalized nuclear trade with India, expanding the country's access to reactor technology and fuel from suppliers in other countries. India has since signed civil nuclear cooperation agreements with the United States, Russia, France, the United Kingdom, South Korea, and Canada, as well as with Argentina, Kazakhstan, Mongolia, and Namibia.[24] The development of foreign supply relationships has helped remedy India's shortage in uranium fuel and has also given the country greater access to intellectual property.

New Delhi plans to position its industry as a major player in the global supply chain, as well as use its expertise in fast reactors and the thorium fuel cycle to become a world leader in nuclear technology.[25] However, achievement of these goals will be impeded by domestic law such as the Nuclear Liability Act, which diverges from international practice in enabling broad legal recourse against suppliers. Private-sector companies, including Indian companies, are at particular risk in the unlimited-liability scenario created by the Act.

RUSSIA

In 2012, nuclear energy was used to generate 166.6 billion kWh in Russia—about 18 percent of the country's overall electricity supply. Nuclear electricity output has grown considerably over the past decade due to improved plant performance, with capacity factors rising from 56 percent in 1998 to 80 percent in 2012.[26]

Russia has an installed nuclear capacity of 23.2 GWe, with 32 operational reactors at 10 locations.[27] The Russian government has stated that it intends to increase nuclear and hydropower generation in the future to allow for greater export of natural gas; current plans call for a doubling of nuclear output—such that nuclear accounts for up to 25 percent of total generation—by 2030.[28] At that point, Russia's installed nuclear capacity would total about 50 GWe.[29]

All of the new nuclear power plants being constructed in Russia are based on indigenous technology. Russia has long been a leader in developing nuclear technology, and Russian-designed reactors can be found in many nations that were once part of the Soviet Union, as well as in several Asian countries. Russia continues to aggressively seek export markets for its reactor designs and nuclear fuel cycle services. This includes plans to build seven or eight floating

---

[22] Ibid.
[23] Business Standard, "India signs safeguards agreement with IAEA," May 2013, http://business-standard.com/india/news/india-signs-safeguards-agreementiaea/347861/.
[24] See "India, South Korea ink civil nuclear deal," *Time of India*, July 25, 2011, http://articles.timesofindia.indiatimes.com/2011-07-25/india/29811954_1_nuclear-cooperation-agreement-nuclear-energy-bilateral-agreement; and "Indian and UK sign nuclear cooperation accord," World Nuclear News, February 12, 2010, http://www.world-nuclear-news.org/NP-India_and_UK_sign_cooperation_accord-1202105.html.
[25] World Nuclear Association, "Nuclear Power in India." http://www.world-nuclear.org/info/inf53.html.
[26] International Atomic Energy Agency, Power Reactor Information System, http://www.iaea.org/PRIS/home.aspx.
[27] U.S. Energy Information Administration, "Russia," http://www.eia.gov/countries/cab.cfm?fips=RS.
[28] World Nuclear Association, "Nuclear Power in Russia." http://www.world-nuclear.org/info/Country-Profiles/Countries-O-S/Russia--Nuclear-Power/#.UZEvNpWsEzU.
[29] "Global Commercial Nuclear Power Capacity Outlook for 2030," McKinsey & Company, February 2012

nuclear power plants by 2015, based on Russia's extensive experience with designing and building nuclear-powered icebreakers.[30]

SOUTH KOREA

South Korea currently ranks sixth in the world in terms of total nuclear-generating capacity (nuclear energy accounts for approximately one-third of the country's overall electricity supply mix). South Korea recently added two new reactors to its grid, bringing its total reactor fleet to 23. Plans for further expansion of the country's nuclear capacity (to as much as 50 percent of overall generation) have not been affected by Fukushima; the government reaffirmed its nuclear strategy in mid-2011, and construction of several new units was launched in 2012. At this point, nine additional reactors are scheduled to be completed by 2021.

A peripheral player in the global nuclear marketplace until recently, South Korea is now a formidable competitor. The start of construction of two new domestic reactors in 2012 was hailed by the South Korean Ministry of Knowledge Economy as a "turning point" for the country's nuclear program because all domestic-made components were used "in the most important areas" of the plant. Developing a domestic capacity to both design nuclear plants and manufacture major components clearly helped South Korea's KEPCO secure the $20-billion United Arab Emirates (UAE) contract to build four 1,400-megawatt units at the end of 2009—an event that sent shockwaves throughout the global nuclear marketplace.

A CHANGING BALANCE OF POWER

The shifting outlook for nuclear power development globally could lead to a major change in the international "balance of power" in nuclear energy and technology. Whereas the United States currently has about 25 percent of the world's nuclear-generating capacity, by 2030 this number could drop nearly in half, to 14 percent.[31] China could displace the United States as the world's largest producer of nuclear energy by that date, and the four nations of China, India, South Korea, and Russia could account for nearly half of total global capacity.

---

[30] World Nuclear Association, "Nuclear Power in Russia." http://www.world-nuclear.org/info/Country-Profiles/Countries-O-S/Russia--Nuclear-Power/#.UZEvNpWsEzU.

[31] "Global Commercial Nuclear Power Capacity Outlook for 2030," McKinsey & Company, February 2012.

Projected Installed Global Nuclear Generating Capacity - 2030

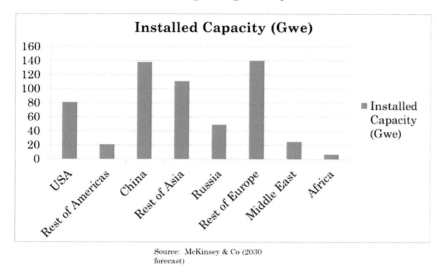

Source: McKinsey & Co (2030 forecast)

Looking further ahead to 2050, the shift could be even more dramatic. Without a marked change in the economics of nuclear power in the United States, domestic nuclear-generating capacity could fall to less than 10 GWe. Assuming China, India, Russia, and South Korea, along with several new entrants, continue to construct and operate new plants, the United States could account for just a few percent of the world's installed commercial nuclear power capacity by mid-century.

In contrast to the outlook for U.S. commercial nuclear generation, the U.S. Navy has given no indication that it plans to scale back or end its reliance on nuclear power for submarines and aircraft carriers. In addition to the Gerald R. Ford class of aircraft carriers discussed earlier, the Navy is also building the next-generation attack submarine, the Virginia class. A total of nearly twenty Virginia-class submarines have been christened, are under construction, or are under contract;[32] each is expected to have an operating life of 30-plus years.

Later chapters of this report discuss the implications of these developments for U.S. economic, energy, and national security and the basis for our concern that a diminished presence in domestic and global markets means a diminished U.S. voice and influence in future international developments concerning nuclear fuel, processing, safety standards, and efforts to address weapons proliferation and security risks. Moreover, this decline in U.S. influence could be exacerbated by post-Fukushima developments in Japan's nuclear energy program, given the close relationships that exist between several major Japanese and American nuclear companies and the history of collaboration between both countries' governments on international nuclear policy matters.

This interdependence, in fact, has increased in recent years as U.S. and Japanese vendors have entered into a growing number of commercial partnerships. For example, Toshiba of Japan purchased Westinghouse in October 2006. The Toshiba Group supplied a significant percentage of the 430-plus units in operation globally. Also, the Japanese and American companies Hitachi and General Electric formed several joint ventures in 2007, including Hitachi-GE Nuclear Energy Limited for the Japanese market and GE-Hitachi Nuclear Energy for the U.S. market. Mitsubishi Nuclear Energy Systems, Inc., a wholly owned subsidiary of Mitsubishi Heavy Industries, is headquartered in Arlington, Virginia. Close engagement is not limited to the reactor and

---

[32] America's Navy, United States Navy Fact File, http://www.navy.mil/navydata/fact_display.asp?cid=4100&tid=100&ct=4.

equipment sector—in fact, various U.S. and Japanese companies are active along the supply chain. For example, USEC of the United States has historically been a maj Source: Moelis uranium to Japan. And Japan Steel Works and Ishikawajima-Harima Heavy Industries (IHI) of Japan have been key manufacturers of reactor vessels for U.S.-led projects globally.

A close alignment of business interests between the U.S. and Japanese nuclear industries is behind a series of efforts by the two governments to conclude nuclear cooperation agreements with potential market countries in recent years. A potential customer country must have bilateral cooperation agreements in place with both the U.S. and Japanese governments if a project by a Japan-U.S. consortium is to proceed in that market. For example, the United States has concluded what are commonly referred to as "123 Agreements" [33] with India (2008), Russia (2008), Turkey (2000),[34] and the United Arab Emirates (2009) in recent years. Additionally, the United States will negotiate, renegotiate, or extend approximately 10 nuclear cooperation agreements in the next three years.[35] Meanwhile, Japan has also concluded nuclear cooperation agreements with Jordan (2010), Russia (2009), South Korea (2010), and Vietnam (2011); all of these agreements were approved by the Japanese parliament in December 2011. Japan has also resumed negotiations on bilateral nuclear cooperation with India.[36]

OTHER NUCLEAR FUEL CYCLE FACILITIES AND CAPABILITIES

Much of the above discussion has focused on reactors and nuclear electricity generating capacity. Other aspects of the nuclear fuel cycle, however, also have important strategic, economic, and national security implications. Uranium enrichment (the "front end" of the nuclear fuel cycle) and spent fuel reprocessing (the "back end" of the nuclear fuel cycle) are of particular concern since both involve technologies and capabilities that could be diverted for weapons applications. A global expansion of nuclear generating capacity will drive increased demand for reactor fuel (enriched uranium, plutonium, or thorium); and it will generate increased quantities of spent fuel to be managed, either through direct disposal or through a combination of reprocessing (to extract some still useful components of the spent fuel) and long-term disposal.

To provide fuel for most types of commercial nuclear reactors, mined uranium has to be first purified and then "enriched" to increase the amount of fissionable uranium-235 it contains. Most light-water reactors in use or planned in the United States and worldwide today require fuel with a U-235 concentration anywhere from 3 to 5 percent. Nuclear weapons require more highly enriched uranium—typically with a U-235 content of 80–95 percent. The methods used to enrich uranium are well developed; those in use today rely on gaseous diffusion or centrifuge technology. Commercial deployment of laser enrichment technologies is possible later this decade.

As shown in the below chart, uranium ore is widely distributed across the globe, with large ore concentrations in nations such as Australia, Kazakhstan, and Canada and with large quantities

---

[33] U.S. nuclear cooperation agreements are commonly referred to as the "123 Agreements" because Section 123 of the Atomic Energy Act mandates a nuclear cooperation agreement to meet nine nonproliferation criteria and directs the president to submit such agreement for congressional approval.

[34] The U.S.-Turkey bilateral agreement was concluded in 2000, with an initial effective period of 15 years, but the cooperation did not begin until 2008.

[35] Paul K. Kerr et al., "Nuclear Energy Cooperation with Foreign Countries: Issues for Congress," Congressional Research Service, July 11, 2011, p. 2.

[36] Anirban Bhaumik, "Indian hopes to restart nuclear talks with Japan soon," *Deccan Herald*, January 26, 2013, http://www.deccanherald.com/content/307958/india-hopes-restart-nuclear-talks.html.

Paducah Gaseous Diffusion Plant

(but in low concentrations) contained in seawater. By contrast, uranium enrichment facilities have been constructed in fewer than a dozen nations.

During the 1960s, the U.S. operated the first uranium enrichment facilities wholly dedicated to the production of low-enriched uranium (LEU) for commercial purposes.[37] Today, the single U.S.-based enrichment company, USEC, accounts for only about 20 percent of global production capacity for enriched uranium.[38]

Instead of being made from uranium enriched in the United States, much of the fuel used in U.S. reactors is fabricated from imported enriched uranium obtained by USEC under a successful agreement with the Russian government to supply down-blended highly enriched uranium—a contract that expires in 2013. Accordingly, USEC announced in 2011 that it had signed a multiyear contract with the Russian firm Techsnabexport for a 10-year supply of commercially produced Russian low-enriched uranium. USEC intends to deliver the uranium to USEC's customers under its portfolio of contracts.

Recently, USEC announced the end of uranium enrichment at its only operating plant in Paducah, Kentucky, which used 50-year-old gaseous diffusion enrichment technology and was too inefficient to compete against foreign suppliers.[39] Although USEC plans to replace the aging Paducah plant with a plant using advanced U.S. centrifuge enrichment technology, prospects for following through on this plan are far from certain.[40] USEC is currently pursuing development of its centrifuge capability under a research, demonstration, and development (RD&D) agreement with the DOE. The objective of the RD&D effort is to demonstrate the technology through construction and operation of a commercial plant configuration 120-centrifuge machine cascade.

In contrast to USEC's diminishing role, the European uranium enrichment company, Urenco, has deployed its centrifuge technology at three locations in Europe, at an operating facility in Hobbs, New Mexico, and (under a joint venture agreement) at a facility planned to be constructed by AREVA in Idaho Falls, Idaho. This will enable Urenco to increase its market share worldwide. In

---

[37] M. D. Laughter, "Profile of World Uranium Enrichment Programs—2009", Global Nuclear Security Technology Division International Safeguards Group, April 2009, http://www.fas.org/nuke/guide/enrich.pdf.
[38] Ibid.; and World Nuclear Association, "Uranium Enrichment," 2013, http://www.world-nuclear.org/info/inf28.html.
[39] John K. Welch, CEO, USEC, "Remarks to Shareholders," April 26, 2012, http://www.usec.com/news/remarks-shareholders-1.
[40] For example, see Gregory Korte, "Politics stands in the way of nuclear plant's future," USA Today, April 27, 2012, http://www.usatoday.com/money/industries/energy/story/2012-04-13/usec-centrifuges-loan-guarantees/54560118/1.

addition, Russia is taking steps to modernize and expand its enrichment services capability, with plans to increase total enrichment capacity by about 50 percent by 2020.[41] China, which currently has two commercial-sized enrichment plants supplied by Russia to provide fuel for civilian reactors,[42] plans an even larger expansion of its enrichment capacity, from about 1,300 separative work units (SWU) today to between 6,000 and 8,000 SWU by 2030. All told, the U.S. share of global exports for enriched uranium and other sensitive nuclear materials declined from approximately 29 percent in 1994 to 10 percent in 2008.[43]

A second U.S. company, General Electric (GE), is attempting to enter the uranium enrichment market through the commercial application of an Australian laser enrichment technology known as SILEX, and on September 25, 2012, NRC staff issued a construction and operating license for the facility (for "separation of isotopes by laser excitation").[44] Laser enrichment holds the potential to be substantially more energy efficient than the gas centrifuge technology in use today. GE is planning to conduct the project in two phases, a test phase and a commercial-scale enrichment plant phase. The NRC issued a construction and operating license for the commercial-scale plant phase on September 25, 2012.[45] In 2008, GE announced the selection of Wilmington, North Carolina, as the site for the construction of the commercial facility.[46] In response to a DOE request for expressions of interest in potential uses for the Paducah gaseous diffusion plant site, GE also indicated a potential interest in that site as a possible location for a laser enrichment facility.[47], [48] However, GE has not announced a construction commitment or timetable.

Increasingly, other countries are also ahead of the United States when it comes to developing and implementing solutions for the back end of the nuclear fuel cycle. The back end of the fuel cycle refers to what happens to spent nuclear fuel once it leaves the reactor. Spent fuel contains quantities of uranium and plutonium that could be reused as reactor fuel, as well as other radioactive by-products of the fission reactions that occurred in the reactor core. There are effectively two options for spent nuclear fuel. The first option is to simply dispose of the spent fuel—presumably in a deep geologic repository designed to isolate the radioactive materials in the fuel over the millennia-long timescales needed for those materials to decay to the point where they no longer present a threat to living organisms. The second option is to reprocess the spent fuel so as to separate the still-usable elements; those elements can then be fabricated into new reactor fuel while the remaining radioactive material is repackaged for permanent disposal. Importantly, both pathways require permanent disposal capability as well as interim storage

---

[41] World Nuclear Association, "Russia's Nuclear Fuel Cycle," http://www.world-nuclear.org/info/inf45a_Russia_nuclear_fuel_cycle.html.
[42] Ibid.
[43] U.S. Government Accountability Office (GAO), "Governmentwide Strategy Could Help Increase Commercial Benefits from U.S. Nuclear Cooperation Agreements with Other Countries," GAO-11-36, November 2010, p. 12, http://www.gao.gov/new.items/d1136.pdf.
[44] Nuclear Regulatory Commission, "GE Laser Enrichment Facility Licensing," http://www.nrc.gov/materials/fuel-cycle-fac/laser.html.
[45] Ibid.
[46] General Electric, Press Release, "GE Hitachi Nuclear Energy Selects Wilmington, N.C. as Site for Potential Commercial Uranium Enrichment Facility," May 1, 2008, http://www.genewscenter.com/content/detail.aspx?releaseid=3471&newsareaid=2.
[47] FedBizOpps.gov, "Request for Expression of Interest in DOE Paducah Gaseous Diffusion Plant," https://www.fbo.gov/index?s=opportunity&mode=form&id=ff41cfd2dd03365797d225a2773629a2&tab=core&_cview =1.
[48] See "Global Laser Enrichment Formally Proposes Uranium Facility for Paducah," March 7, 2013, http://nsspi.tamu.edu/pauloscornerarticles/2013-03/global-laser-enrichment-formally-proposes-uranium-facility-for-paducah.

facilities to allow spent fuel to cool off for further handling after it has been removed from the reactor core.

Around the world, the great majority of commercial nuclear reactors are light-water reactors operating on the "once-through" fuel cycle—that is, the enriched uranium that fuels the reactor is used once and then stored pending final disposal. The assumption in the early days of the U.S. nuclear program was that spent fuel would be reprocessed, but the United States abandoned commercial reprocessing in the 1970s—initially out of concern about the potential for nuclear weapons proliferation and later also for economic reasons. Today, a handful of countries still engage in reprocessing (see table below); several more, including China, have announced plans to develop reprocessing capability for civil nuclear applications.[49]

From a national security and weapons proliferation standpoint, the technologies and facilities needed to reprocess spent nuclear fuel and fabricate recycled fuel—like the technologies and facilities needed to enrich uranium—present special concerns and risks. This is because they all involve the handling of materials and the development of expertise that could be diverted for weapons applications. Various international mechanisms and regimes have been established to attempt to constrain that possibility—notably the IAEA and the Treaty on the Non-Proliferation of Nuclear Weapons (NPT)—but those mechanisms and regimes offer at best imperfect safeguards, as current concerns over the nuclear programs of Iran and North Korea illustrate.

Regardless of a nation's plans for reprocessing spent nuclear fuel, a final disposal facility will be required to manage long-lived radioactive wastes, though Finland and Sweden are in the process of doing so. No nation has yet succeeded in establishing a final disposal capacity for spent nuclear fuel or high-level radioactive wastes. In this context, the ability of the United States to demonstrate a viable path toward the licensing and construction of a deep geologic repository could help emerging nations decide to pursue a once-through fuel cycle rather than pursue reprocessing as part of an overall waste-management strategy. Yet the U.S. administration's decision to halt the Yucca Mountain project has eroded the U.S. position

World commercial reprocessing capacity[58]

		(tonnes per year)
LWR fuel	France, La Hague	1700
	UK, Sellafield (THORP)	900
	Russia, Ozersk (Mayak)	400
	Japan (Rokkasho)	800*
	Total LWR (approx)	3800
Other nuclear fuels	UK, Sellafield (Magnox)	1500
	India (PHWR, 4 plants)	330
	Total other (approx)	1830
Total civil capacity		5630

---

[49] Associated Press, "China Ready to Reprocess Nuclear Fuel," *New York Times*, January 3, 2011, http://www.nytimes.com/2011/01/04/world/asia/04china.html?_r=1.

as the clear leader in geologic repository development. To be sure, the U.S. experience in preparing a license application for the Yucca Mountain site and in developing and operating the Waste Isolation Pilot Plant for deep geologic disposal of transuranic wastes keeps the United States quite relevant in waste-management discussions. But today, nations such as Sweden and Finland are ahead of the United States in spent-fuel disposal and exercise increasing influence over the waste-management directions taken by other nations.

Chapter 2

MAKING THE CASE: THE NATIONAL INTEREST AND U.S. NUCLEAR ENERGY LEADERSHIP

The health of the U.S. civil nuclear industry bears directly on our nation's ability to advance a number of crucial objectives, particularly with respect to nonproliferation, military strength, and energy security. At the same time, a robust nuclear industry helps advance several important domestic priorities, such as reducing greenhouse gas emissions while creating jobs and supplying affordable, reliable energy.

ADVANCING NONPROLIFERATION OBJECTIVES

From the 1950s through the 1980s, the United States dominated the international market for commercial nuclear technology. As the dominant supplier, the United States was able to exert great influence in shaping the global nuclear nonproliferation regime. A strong program of domestic nuclear plant operation and construction, combined with government policies to promote advanced technologies and support nuclear technology cooperation with, and exports to, other nations helped the United States sustain this leadership position for decades.[50]

A particularly important source of U.S. leverage in the past was the ability to provide nuclear technology, fuel, and services to other countries on a reliable and stable basis, while imposing strict nonproliferation conditions.[51] These U.S.-imposed controls and conditions go beyond the limitations in the Treaty on the Non-Proliferation of Nuclear Weapons (commonly known as the NPT) and include nine criteria that an agreement with a nonnuclear weapon state must meet. As described in a recent Congressional Research Service report titled "Nuclear Cooperation with Other Countries: A Primer," these criteria include "guarantees that:

- Safeguards on transferred nuclear material and equipment continue in perpetuity;
- Full-scope International Atomic Energy Agency (IAEA) safeguards are applied in non-nuclear weapon states;
- Nothing transferred is used for any nuclear explosive device or for any other military purpose;
- The United States has the right to demand the return of transferred nuclear materials and equipment, as well as any special nuclear material produced through their use, if the cooperating state detonates a nuclear explosive device or terminates or abrogates an IAEA safeguards agreement;
- There is no retransfer of material or classified data without U.S. consent;
- Physical security on nuclear material is maintained;
- There is no enrichment or reprocessing by the recipient state of transferred nuclear material or nuclear material produced with materials or facilities transferred pursuant to the agreement without prior approval;
- Storage for transferred plutonium and highly enriched uranium is approved in advance by the United States; and

---

[50] Ibid.
[51] Ibid.

- Any material or facility produced or constructed through use of special nuclear technology transferred under the cooperation agreement is subject to all of the above requirements."[52]

Today, due largely to the fact that no new nuclear power plant has been built in the United States for more than three decades, our nuclear industrial capabilities have eroded. As prospects for a new surge of nuclear investment in the United States have dimmed, a number of U.S. firms have been selling off their nuclear capabilities. Meanwhile, as discussed in the previous chapter, several other countries are pursuing ambitious nuclear power programs and are poised to become major international suppliers.[53] In particular, France, Japan, South Korea, and Russia, with China close behind, have developed significant bases of operational experience and are able to compete effectively with their U.S.-based counterparts. While administration officials correctly argue that "nuclear trade carries with it a critical nonproliferation advantage in the form of consent rights, along with other opportunities to influence the nuclear policies of our partners," such trade is not possible unless U.S. firms can offer something other nations want to buy.[54]

Current trends are especially concerning from a national security standpoint because much of the recent global upsurge of interest in nuclear power is occurring in parts of the world that are less responsive to U.S. policies and prerogatives. To exert a positive influence on the nuclear development and nonproliferation policies, especially of these countries, the United States needs to be in a position to act as an active supplier and partner in the evolution of these countries' programs.

CONTROLLING THE SPREAD OF ENRICHMENT AND REPROCESSING TECHNOLOGIES

Growth in nuclear electricity production outside the United States will drive a commensurate increase in the demand for enriched uranium (or for plutonium recovered from used fuel via some form of reprocessing). Inevitably, the facilities needed to supply this demand—because they can be used to produce both nuclear fuel and nuclear weapons-usable material—are of particular concern from a national security standpoint.

During the 1960s, the United States supplied a significant percentage of the market for uranium enrichment services outside the former Soviet Union, through government-owned uranium enrichment plants located in Ohio, Kentucky, and Tennessee (Oak Ridge). The United States was also a major supplier of uranium. At its peak in 1979, employment in the U.S. uranium industry was nearly 22,000 person-years.[55] Employment in 2011 was 1,191 person-years,[56] only about 5 percent of the employment level in this industry in the 1970s. Meanwhile, domestic uranium production has fallen, for reasons discussed in the previous chapter, to about 11 percent of the 1980 production level.[57]

In addition to determined efforts by Urenco (the European enrichment company) as well as China and Russia to expand their commercial enrichment capabilities (see discussion in previous

---

[52] Paul K. Kerr and Mary Beth Nikitin, "Nuclear Cooperation with Other Countries: A Primer," Congressional Research Service, June 19, 2012, p. 2, http://www.fas.org/sgp/crs/nuke/RS22937.pdf.
[53] Ibid., p. 1.
[54] Letter from Daniel B. Poneman and Ellen O. Tauscher to Senator John Kerry, Chairman, Committee of Foreign Relations, January 10, 2012.
[55] Ibid.
[56] U.S. Energy Information Administration, "Domestic Uranium Production Report–Annual," May 9, 2012, http://www.eia.gov/uranium/production/annual/.
[57] Ibid.

chapter), several additional countries, such as Argentina, Brazil, India, Iran, Japan, and Pakistan, have small enrichment capabilities. Enrichment plants in India and Pakistan lack safeguards and many believe that Iran's enrichment capabilities are intended to support a weapons program, despite the efforts of the International Atomic Energy Agency (IAEA) to apply nonproliferation safeguards. The North Koreans are known to have at least one enrichment plant and there are reasons to believe they might have more such facilities. Other countries, while not currently operating enrichment facilities, have made clear that they do not intend to forego their rights under the NPT to do so in the future.[58]

In a recent paper titled "Limiting Transfers of Enrichment and Reprocessing Technology: Issues, Constraints and Options," Fred McGoldrick, an expert in nuclear security and nonproliferation, describes several ways in which the diffusion of enrichment technologies can increase the risk of nuclear weapons proliferation[59]:

> "First, enrichment facilities can produce nuclear materials—highly enriched uranium (HEU)—that are directly usable in nuclear weapons. With such materials, a state could abrogate its nonproliferation commitments and produce a nuclear weapon within a short period of time. Given the legal ability of a party to the NPT to acquire enrichment (and reprocessing) facilities, produce weapon-usable materials and then withdraw from the Treaty after giving notice of its withdrawal three months in advance, a state would be free to develop nuclear weapons without, strictly speaking, violating the NPT.
>
> Second, it is difficult to detect, either through national technical means or international inspections or both, clandestine enrichment plants using such technologies as centrifuge or laser isotope separation.
>
> Third, having enrichment capability could increase the chance that nuclear weapons advocates could convince leaders of a state to develop nuclear weapons. Other states fearing such an outcome may be tempted to build "standby" capabilities of their own. (In this regard a strong distinction should be made with power reactors, for which there is little evidence that a decision to proceed with a nuclear energy program increases the probability of a state deciding also to pursue a nuclear weapons program.)
>
> Finally, highly enriched uranium produced at enrichment plants offers a tempting target for terrorists or other non-state actors."

The potential for the spread of reprocessing technology raises similar proliferation concerns. While the United States. does not reprocess commercial reactor fuel, several leading nuclear nations—including France, Russia, and Japan—do. China[60] and India[61] are both conducting reprocessing on a limited scale and could expand their use of reprocessing technology in the future.

Reprocessing in France and Russia (and past reprocessing in the United Kingdom) has led to the accumulation of large stocks of separated plutonium that is intended for reuse in reactors but that

---

[58] Ibid., p. 10.
[59] ibid., p. 1.
[60] World Nuclear Association, "China's Nuclear Fuel Cycle," April 2013, http://www.world-nuclear.org/info/inf63b_china_nuclearfuelcycle.html.
[61] Fred McGoldrick, *Limiting Transfers of Enrichment and Reprocessing Technology: Issues, Constraints and Opinions*, Belfer Center for Science and International Affairs, Harvard Kennedy School, May 2011. http://belfercenter.ksg.harvard.edu/files/MTA-NSG-report-color.pdf.

has not been converted into fuel form.[62] There are many reasons why the supply of separated plutonium has outpaced demand, including technical challenges associated with the use of plutonium fuel in today's reactors and the slower-than-expected development of "advanced" reactors that can more readily use plutonium as fuel. But regardless of the reasons, experience has shown that nations that engage in large-scale reprocessing can wind up having to manage and secure large quantities of weapons-usable materials. While this isn't necessarily a cause for alarm in the nations that are presently managing these stockpiles, the obvious concern is that nations that are not presently nuclear weapons states could engage in reprocessing—as allowed under the NPT—and accumulate plutonium inventories that could be readily diverted to a nuclear weapons program.

National Stocks of Separated Plutonium

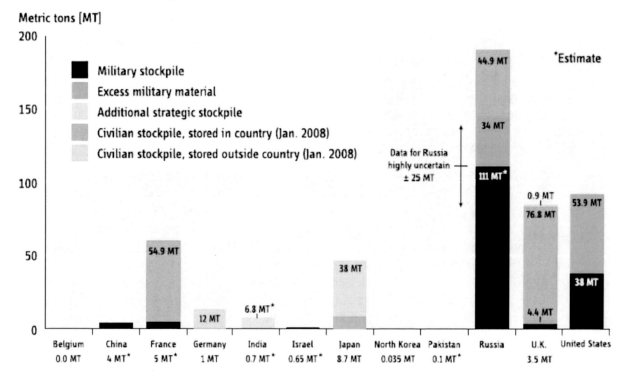

[62] International Panel on Fissile Materials, "Global Fissile Material Report 2009: A Path to Nuclear Disarmament," 2009, p. 15, http://fissilematerials.org/library/gfmr09.pdf.

Concerns regarding the potential misuse of enrichment and reprocessing capabilities have long been the basis for U.S. efforts to halt the spread of these technologies. One of the most significant developments in the history of efforts to achieve this objective came in the late 1970s, when the major nuclear suppliers agreed to form the Nuclear Suppliers Group (NSG). The NSG established guidelines governing exports of nuclear materials, equipment, and technology. In addition, members agreed to exercise restraint in the transfer of sensitive materials and technology, and specifically to establish special controls on the spread of enrichment and reprocessing technology.[63]

Unfortunately, past performance is no guarantee of future success. The fact remains that nonnuclear weapon states have a right to enrichment and reprocessing technology under the NPT.[64] If the United States were to develop and deploy a competitive uranium enrichment technology, international demand for this technology might put the United States in a stronger position to seek nonproliferation assurances from recipient nations that go beyond what is required by the NPT (and beyond what is required under NSG guidelines). Currently, however, America's role as a supplier of uranium enrichment services and technology looks set to decline, along with U.S. engagement in global markets for nuclear technology more generally. This will likely mean a loss of leverage in persuading aspiring nuclear nations to refrain from reprocessing.

SUPPORT FOR OUR NATIONAL DEFENSE CAPABILITIES

As discussed in Chapter 1, the U.S. civil nuclear industry has long supported, and been supported by, the U.S. Navy's nuclear propulsion program.

In fact, the commercial U.S. nuclear power industry is a direct descendant of the naval nuclear propulsion program. The U.S. Atomic Energy Commission (AEC) was established after World War II and subsequently took the lead in research and development to advance nuclear-powered energy generation. Momentum for this program built in 1949 when U.S. Navy Captain Hyman Rickover established a division in the AEC to develop a nuclear power plant for a submarine. This submarine reactor technology formed the basis for larger nuclear power reactor designs, and in the mid-1950s, the Duquesne Light Company of Pittsburgh, Pennsylvania, agreed to build and operate a conventional steam-driven power-generation system using nuclear reactor technology provided by the U.S. Navy. The resulting facility at Shippingport, Pennsylvania, is widely regarded as launching the first generation of commercial nuclear power plants in the United States.[65]

[63] Ibid., p. 1.
[64] Ibid., p. 19.
[65] The Babcock & Wilcox Company, *Steam: Its Generation and Use*, Edition 41.

Ultimately, the two main reactor technologies developed for naval use—pressurized water reactors and boiling water reactors—were commercialized by U.S. firms and later sold to other countries around the world.

To this day, the Navy and the commercial U.S. nuclear industry rely on many of the same providers of nuclear equipment and specialized manufacturing capability. While the Navy is careful to develop sources of supply that can weather short-term ups and downs, a sustained decline in the number of U.S. firms able to provide these products and services could leave the Navy with little choice but to rely more heavily on foreign suppliers, or even begin to invest in and develop its own dedicated supply chain resources.

Finally, a declining domestic commercial nuclear industry could affect the Navy's ability to enlist servicemen and women to serve in its nuclear propulsion program. The program's current recruitment materials assure new sailors that "Your knowledge of traditional and nuclear power will be an asset in high demand, whether with America's Navy or the civilian sector."[66] That pitch may be increasingly hard to make in the context of a contracting nuclear power industry with diminishing employment opportunities.

GLOBAL LEADERSHIP IN SAFETY AND SECURITY STANDARDS

The United States has been regulating applications of nuclear technology longer than any other nation. Starting in 1954, well before the NRC was created, nuclear regulation was the responsibility of the Atomic Energy Commission (AEC). The Atomic Energy Act of 1954, which launched the commercial nuclear power industry in the United States, gave the AEC two functions: to encourage the use of nuclear power while also regulating its safety.

Having a single agency responsible for both the promotion and regulation of nuclear power was understandably viewed as creating the potential for internal conflicts of interest.[67] This situation was rectified in 1974, when President Ford signed the Energy Reorganization Act. The Reorganization Act, among other things, established the Energy Research and Development Agency (ERDA, the forerunner to today's DOE) and replaced the AEC with the NRC. In this way, the two missions of nuclear technology promotion and nuclear technology regulation were separated and allocated to two distinct agencies.[68]

The 1979 accident at Three Mile Island (TMI) led to a wholesale reevaluation of both regulatory and industry approaches to assuring nuclear power plant safety. Shortly after the TMI accident, both the NRC and industry implemented major structural changes to address the problems identified by several groups that examined the event. The industry formed the Institute of Nuclear Power Operations (INPO) to promote the highest levels of safety and reliability in the nuclear power operations. Finally, the industry established the Nuclear Electric Insurance Limited to provide insurance coverage for nuclear plants using rates that were contingent on active participation in INPO and adherence to its standards.[69]

---

[66] See America's Navy, "Serving a Core Function: Nuclear Technicians and Power Pant Operators—Nuclear Operations," http://www.navy.com/careers/nuclear-energy/nuclear-operations.html.
[67] Gary Vine, "Abridged History of Reactor and Fuel Cycle Technologies Development: A White Paper for the Reactor and Fuel Cycle Technology Subcommittee of the Blue Ribbon Commission," March 15, 2011, p. 17.
[68] U.S. Nuclear Regulatory Commission, "History," http://www.nrc.gov/about-nrc/history.html.
[69] Gary Vine, "Abridged History of Reactor and Fuel Cycle Technologies Development," p. 21.

Throughout the 1970s and into the 1980s, the NRC reviewed license applications for, and oversaw the construction, startup, and operation of, more than 100 commercial nuclear power reactors in the United States. Beginning in the 1980s and extending to today, the NRC also reviewed new plant designs and plans to increase the power output of operating reactors. As a result, the NRC has more collective experience than any other nuclear regulatory agency in the world.

Thanks to robust NRC regulation and its own initiatives, particularly including the INPO, the commercial nuclear power industry in the United States has accumulated an impressive record of operational and safety performance. Operational and technological improvements have enabled plant operators to dramatically boost performance over the last several decades. For example, in 1980 the average capacity factor for the commercial U.S. nuclear plant fleet as a whole was just 56.3 percent. This figure rose to 66 percent in 1990 and continued rising over the past two decades, reaching 89 percent in 2011.[70]

For decades, and continuing through today, the U.S. system of regulations and operational standards has been viewed as the best in the world. An NRC license for a particular reactor design has been viewed as the "gold standard" and has opened opportunities to market that design around the world.[71] The desire to learn from U.S. regulatory and operational experiences is one of the factors that caused nations in the past to want to enter into agreements for nuclear cooperation with the United States, and it has given Washington an important edge in negotiating such agreements.

Cooperating with other countries on issues of nuclear safety, in turn, gives the United States an opportunity to shape behaviors in other areas, particularly with respect to plant security, materials safeguards, emergency response, and nonproliferation. Other leading supplier nations don't always adhere to the same strict controls the United States has adopted in these areas. Maintaining an edge in the regulatory arena, however, will be difficult if our nation's own commercial nuclear activities decline.

---

[70] Nuclear Energy Institute, "Resources and Stats," http://www.nei.org/resourcesandstats/graphicsandcharts/performancestatistics/.
[71] Dale E. Klein, Chairman, U.S. Nuclear Regulatory Commission, "Promoting Public Confidence in Nuclear Safety through High Standards," prepared remarks, October 8, 2008, p. 2, http://pbadupws.nrc.gov/docs/ML0828/ML082820479.pdf.

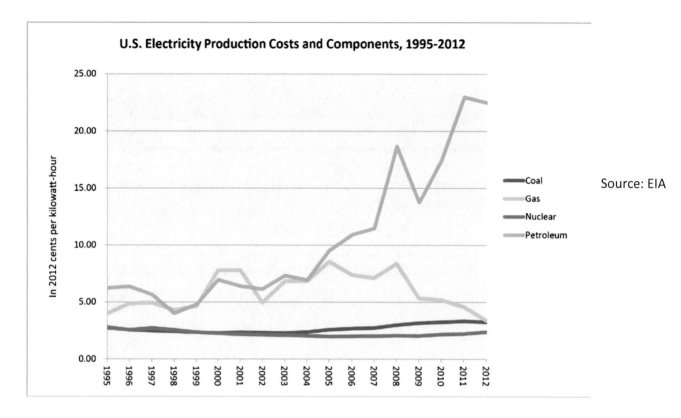

As a large part of the overall U.S. electricity supply mix, nuclear energy provides substantial energy security and fuel diversity benefits.[72] These benefits—coupled with the low operating and maintenance costs of existing nuclear power plants [see figure above]—have helped U.S. utilities deliver reliable electricity at relatively low and stable prices over decades of sustained demand growth.

With the changes that have occurred in electricity markets over the past two decades—particularly the introduction of retail competition in about half the states—energy supply diversity and other long-term, nonmonetary considerations have been deemphasized as electricity providers have shifted their focus to short-term profitability. In regions where electricity supply is still regulated, such as the southeastern United States, these benefits are factored into decisionmaking by utilities and public utility commissions. As a result, nuclear is viewed much more favorably.

The emergence of inexpensive domestic natural gas supplies has made it more difficult for electricity decisionmakers—even those in the Southeast—to take a long view and assign value to the energy diversity and security benefits offered by nuclear power. The conventional wisdom is that natural gas prices will remain low throughout the decade; current price forecasts reflect that assumption. But it's important to recognize that these are just forecasts; nobody can say with certainty what impact more stringent environmental regulations, public concern about natural gas drilling (especially hydraulic fracturing or "fracking"), or other market factors (including the potential development of a major export market for U.S.-produced gas) will have on future gas

---

[72] Presentation by Gerry Cauley, president and CEO, North American Electric Reliability Corporation, January 2012.

prices and on future gas price volatility. By contrast, electricity production costs at existing nuclear reactors have been remarkably stable over the last several decades, because these production costs are largely immune from changes in the price of uranium. Even when uranium prices climbed well above recent norms, as they did in the late 2000s, fuel costs still accounted for less than 15 percent of the price of nuclear-generated electricity.[73] In fact, once a nuclear plant is built, its operating costs can be forecast with a far higher degree of certainty than in the case of coal or natural gas-fired generators.

Finally, America's nuclear energy infrastructure contributes to U.S. security in one additional, less obvious, but clearly important way. In many parts of the country, nuclear plants anchor the electric grid and help to assure the continuous, reliable availability of affordable, high-quality electricity services on which our economy—and our defense systems—depend. As these plants retire, large quantities of new baseload capacity will be needed to assure continued grid stability.

ENVIRONMENTAL BENEFITS

Nuclear energy is currently the only commercially available, low-carbon generating resource that can provide reliable baseload power on a large scale. Any scenario for achieving substantial global carbon reductions in the future will require bringing large increments of low-carbon capacity on line, in the United States and worldwide. This could be much more difficult and potentially much more expensive without a sizable contribution from nuclear energy.

Political will to act on climate change has recently waned in the United States and elsewhere. But these conditions could change quickly if warming trends accelerate or if evidence emerges that the global climate system could be nearing a kind of tipping point beyond which damages become much more difficult or costly to manage.

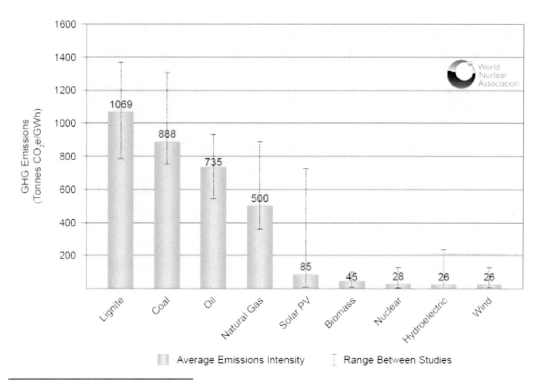

_____

[73] World Nuclear Association, "The Economics of Nuclear Power," March 2013, http://www.world-nuclear.org/info/inf02.html.

At present, nuclear energy accounts for about two-thirds of the low-carbon electricity supply in the United States and about 45 percent of the low-carbon electricity supply globally.[74] Over the next several decades, access to improved nuclear technologies could have enormous option value for reconciling the energy needs of modern societies with the scale and pace of carbon reductions needed to avert the most damaging consequences of human-induced warming. Indeed, access to U.S.-origin nuclear power technology could even be an important bargaining chip for U.S. negotiators if the United States someday finds itself in the position of bringing other countries along in an international effort to limit greenhouse gas emissions.

JOB CREATION AND OTHER ECONOMIC BENEFITS

Beyond its fuel diversity and energy security benefits, nuclear power provides significant regional and local benefits. Many nuclear plants have the support of their host communities because of the jobs they sustain, the tax revenues they generate, and the demand they create for high-quality components that require sophisticated manufacturing capability.

In particular, new nuclear plant construction supports large numbers of highly skilled and well-paid manufacturing jobs in the sectors that supply specialized plant components. According to one study of the job impacts associated with a large-scale program of new-plant construction, "this represents the most significant benefit to the wider economy, particularly when compared with the alternative of construction of fossil fuel plants. By retaining or repatriating these skilled functions, the United States will be at the leading edge of nuclear expertise within the global economy. This creates a potential source of future export earnings as the US provides expertise to select countries expanding their nuclear energy capacity."[75]

A 2012 study conducted by the Nuclear Energy Institute looked more closely at the economic and employment impacts of individual nuclear power plants.[76] That study concluded that the average nuclear power plant employs between 400 and 700 people to operate the plant (plus an undisclosed but significant number for plant security) and generates more than $25 billion in local economic value over the life of the plant.

On a per-megawatt basis, nuclear plants create far more local employment than nearly any other source of large-scale electricity generation.[77]

---

[74] U.S. Energy Information Administration, "Short-Term Energy Outlook," May 7, 2013, http://205.254.135.7/forecasts/steo/report/electricity.cfm.

[75] Oxford Economics, "Economic, Employment and Environmental Benefits of Renewed U.S. Investment in Nuclear Energy: National and State Analysis," 2008, p. 4, http://www.oxfordeconomics.com/publication/open/222534.

[76] http://www.nei.org/CorporateSite/media/filefolder/NuclearEnergy's-Energy-s-Economic-Benefits--Current-and-Future: http://www.nei.org/resourcesandstats/Documentlibrary/New-Plants/whitepaper/jobs.pdf?ext=.pdf.

[77] Donald Harker and Peter Hans Hirschboeck, "Green Job Realities," *Public Utilities Fortnightly*, May 2010, http://www.fortnightly.com/fortnightly/2010/05/green-job-realities.

Chapter 3

CHALLENGES FOR THE U.S. NUCLEAR ENERGY INDUSTRY

This chapter explores the key challenges that must be addressed to secure a strong future for the U.S. nuclear energy industry. As such, it lays the groundwork for our recommendations, which follow in Chapter 4:

- Export Market Challenges
    - Difficulties in negotiating nuclear trade agreements
    - Overly burdensome export approval process
    - Insufficient export incentives
    - Technological competitiveness

- Domestic Challenges
    - Affordability of and financial structuring for new plants
    - Need to provide a convincing path forward on nuclear waste
    - Regulatory uncertainty and unpredictability
    - Wavering public and political support

EXPORT MARKET CHALLENGES

Given current patterns of nuclear energy development around the world, the most important opportunities for U.S. nuclear firms over the next several years are likely to be in export markets. However, the U.S. industry faces significant competitive challenges in these markets, despite its longstanding leadership in nuclear products and services. For example, the U.S. Department of Commerce estimates that the international market for nuclear equipment and services will total between $500 and $740 billion over the next 10 years.[78] But U.S. nuclear exports in recent years have remained relatively flat (see figure below). Several factors are at work. One is that U.S. suppliers do not benefit from the same level of government support in overseas markets as do their foreign competitors. Non-U.S. firms typically have the full backing of their national governments, while U.S. firms enjoy only fragmented support and are subject to particularly cumbersome export regulations.

DIFFICULTIES IN NEGOTIATING NUCLEAR TRADE AGREEMENTS

New government-imposed requirements have increased the complexity and difficulty of negotiating nuclear trade agreements with other countries. These changes have created an unintended but significant barrier to stronger U.S. participation in global export markets.

Such agreements, which typically outline the parameters of any future nuclear technology transfers between the United States and a potential recipient country, are a prerequisite for U.S. commercial nuclear exports. They are known in the industry as "123 Agreements" because they are governed by Section 123 of the Atomic Energy Act. The agreements cover "significant nuclear exports," a designation that encompasses power reactors, research reactors, source and special

---

[78] International Trade Administration, "Commerce Report: Small Modular Nuclear Reactors Can Help Meet Future Energy Demands, Create American Jobs," February 16, 2011,

U.S. Civil Nuclear Exports (in thousands of U.S. Dollars)

Product	2008	2009	2010	2011
Enriched Uranium	$1,391,791	$1,761,568	$1,266,016	$1,074,562
Nuclear Reactors	$33,253	$319	$420	$263
Isotropic Separation Machinery	$10,304	$14,258	$6,060	$7,720
Fuel Cartridges	$150,432	$183,760	$343,812	$314,085
Parts of Nuclear Reactors	$88,714	$87,462	$71,634	$96,737
TOTAL:	$1,674,494	$2,047,367	$1,687,942	$1,493,367

Source: USITC
Note: These figures do not include nuclear services or dual-use items.

nuclear materials (for use as reactor fuel), and major components of reactors, including pressure vessels, primary coolant pumps, fuel handling machines and control rod drives.[79]

The U.S. has Section 123 Agreements in place with 21 individual countries, the 27 countries under the EURATOM consortium, Taiwan, and the International Atomic Energy Agency.[80] Seven of these agreements are scheduled to expire by 2015 (including agreements with major trading partners such as China, South Korea, and Taiwan). In addition, the United States does not have agreements in place with several nations that are pursuing new nuclear programs, including Saudi Arabia and Vietnam.[81]

Negotiating and receiving congressional approval for 123 Agreements can take several years, and can be derailed by issues not directly relevant to the agreement. For example, President Bush and Russian president Putin agreed in July 2006 to negotiate an agreement for cooperation, and a signed agreement was submitted to Congress in May 2008.[82] But the agreement was withdrawn by

---

[79] U.S. Department of Commerce, International Trade Administration, "Civil Nuclear Exporters Guide," May 2009, http://ita.doc.gov/td/energy/Civil%20Nuclear%20Exporters%20Guide%20(FINAL).pdf.
[80] U.S. Government Accountability Office, "Governmentwide Strategy Could Help Increase Commercial Benefits from U.S. Nuclear Cooperation Agreements with Other Countries," GAO-11-36, November 2010, p. 1, http://www.gao.gov/new.items/d1136.pdf.
[81] Nuclear Energy Institute, "Public Policy: Nuclear Cooperation Agreements," March 2012, http://www.nei.org/publicpolicy/trade/diplomacy.
[82] Robert Einhorn et al., "The U.S.-Russia Civil Nuclear Agreement: A Framework for Cooperation," Center for Strategic and International Studies, May 2008.

President Bush in August 2008 after the start of the Russia-Georgia war.[83] President Obama resubmitted the agreement for approval in May 2010, and it went into force in January 2011.[84]

CHANGES ARE NEEDED TO THE BURDENSOME EXPORT APPROVAL PROCESS

U.S. nuclear exports are subject to a complex, cumbersome, and time-consuming web of export control regulations that are administered by several federal agencies. These include 10 CFR 810, administered by the Department of Energy (DOE), for exports of technology; 10 CFR 110, administered by the Nuclear Regulatory Commission (NRC), for exports of actual items; and 15 CFR 730-774, administered by the Department of Commerce (DOC), for exports of dual-use technology. Although these regulations play an important role in ensuring that nuclear technology, materials, and components are used exclusively for peaceful purposes, their implementation often confuses and frustrates exporters and customers alike and results in a competitive disadvantage to U.S. firms.

DOE's regulation of nuclear technology. Part 810 controls the provision of assistance to activities that directly or indirectly produce special nuclear material outside the United States. DOE also applies this regulation to "deemed exports," which is the transfer of technology to foreign individuals regardless of location. That means that visits by foreign experts to the United States or sharing information with foreign employees falls under this regulation. Part 810 is broadly interpreted by DOE to apply to technology transfers and technical assistance involving any part of the nuclear fuel cycle.[85] This is commonly applied to designs, sales information, technical specifications, as well as operating information and procedures.

In order for U.S. suppliers to export to certain "restricted" countries—which include India, China, and other important partners in nuclear trade—the Part 810 rule requires that they obtain a specific authorization approval from the secretary of energy. DOE currently requires one year to process the typical specific authorization. Certain cooperation and technology exports are "pre-approved" through a general authorization for some countries. For example, technology transfer related to light water reactors to Mexico is generally authorized.

A Part 810 specific authorization requires nonproliferation assurances from the recipient's government that the transferred technology will be used only for peaceful purposes and not be retransferred without prior U.S. consent. DOE often points to the foreign government as a source of delays in issuing these authorizations. But involvement of multiple U.S. departments and agencies in the review process contributes significantly to the inefficiency.

Equivalent licenses in other nuclear supplier countries are required by law to be processed within strict time limits. Processing times of equivalent licenses in Russia, Japan, and South Korea range from 15 to 90 days. As a result, the Part 810 rule does not just impede U.S. suppliers from holding timely commercial discussions with international customers, it imposes on U.S. suppliers a competitive disadvantage, particularly because many of those transfers are needed prior to an actual new reactor tender.

---

[83] Matthew Rojansky and Peter Topychkanov, "The 123 Nuclear Cooperation Agreement: Energizing the U.S.-Russia Reset," *The Hill*, September 15, 2010, http://thehill.com/blogs/congress-blog/foreign-policy/118899-the-123-nuclear-cooperation-agreement-energizing-the-us-russia-reset.

[84] U.S. Department of State, Fact Sheet, "The Agreement between the Government of the United States of America and the Government of the Russian Federation... (U.S.-Russia 123 Agreement)," http://www.state.gov/r/pa/prs/ps/2011/01/154318.htm.

[85] U.S. Department of Commerce, International Trade Administration, "Civil Nuclear Exporters Guide," May 2009, http://ita.doc.gov/td/energy/Civil%20Nuclear%20Exporters%20Guide%20(FINAL).pdf

NRC's regulation of nuclear items. If a U.S. supplier wishes to export nuclear components, materials, or fuel, an NRC Part 110 license is required. Before a Part 110 license for these exports can be approved, a Section 123 agreement with the customer country needs to be in force. Typically requiring about a year to process, Part 110 licenses are required for the following types of hardware and physical material exports:

- Nuclear production and utilization facilities and especially designed or prepared equipment/components for such facilities
- Special nuclear material
- Source material
- Byproduct material
- Deuterium and heavy water
- Nuclear-grade graphite for nuclear end use[86]

Like the government-to-government assurances required for Part 810 authorizations, obtaining a Part 110 license requires that the recipient government pledge to use the acquired items in accordance with the applicable 123 Agreement.[87]

DOC's regulation of dual-use technology. Finally, the Bureau of Industry and Security (BIS) at the Department of Commerce has jurisdiction over certain nuclear-related "dual-use" items (items that can be used for both civilian and military purposes). Such items can include simulators, detectors, analytic equipment, and many other components.[88] Typically, these licenses are processed within 90 days.

Varying impact on competitiveness. Although Part 810 and Part 110 licenses typically take a year or more to process, the impacts of these delays are significantly different because of the items controlled and when they are required. For example, if a consulting or engineering firm is planning to export technology under 10 CFR 810 to help establish a nuclear program abroad, government approval (license) is often required early in the project development process, and lead time is very limited. If a manufacturer is planning to export a major component under Part 110 for a nuclear project, a license is often required later in the project, providing greater lead time. In fact, the transfer of a component under Part 110 is often preceded years earlier by the transfer of related information under a Part 810 license. DOE also applies Part 810 to proprietary information used for marketing purposes. Such information must be shared early in the tender process, often with little lead time. Long delays in obtaining Part 810 licenses can therefore preclude U.S. suppliers from competition. For these commercial reasons, the processing of Part 810 licenses is significantly more urgent for exporters than the processing of Part 110 licenses.

The entire export approval process is mapped out in the figure below.[89]

Though existing U.S. trade requirements are more restrictive than those of other supplier countries, limited support exists in Congress to require additional provisions that could make it even harder to execute or renew nuclear-related trade agreements in the future. During the last Congress, the House Foreign Affairs Committee unanimously adopted HR 1280, which sought to impose on partner countries several new requirements that are not required by other suppliers, including a condition that the partner forswear enrichment and reprocessing technologies. The

---

[86] Ibid.
[87] Ibid.
[88] Ibid.
[89] Ibid.

bill, which did not receive a vote on the House floor, would have also revised current law by requiring Congress to actively affirm such agreements—via a joint congressional resolution—before taking effect. It remains to be seen whether similar legislation will be introduced in the current Congress.

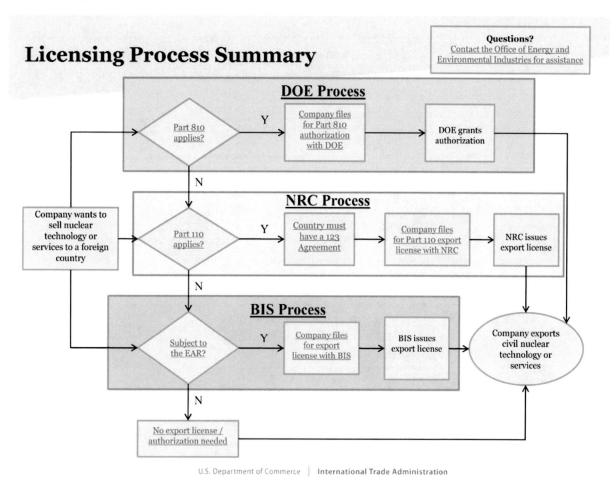

Representative Ros-Lehtinen and other members of Congress want the United States to replicate in future 123 Agreements the same assurances accepted by the UAE as part of a 123 Agreement formalized in 2009. In that agreement, the UAE declared it would not engage in uranium enrichment or reprocessing (commonly referred to as ENR) on UAE soil. At the time, a State Department spokesman branded this pledge the "gold standard" for future U.S. nuclear agreements.[90]

However, administration officials have told Congress that nuclear agreements being negotiated with Vietnam and Jordan might not meet the same "no-ENR" standard. Instead, the administration plans to take a "case-by-case" approach to negotiating future agreements, according to a January 10, 2012, letter from the deputy secretary of energy, Daniel Poneman, and the undersecretary of state for arms control and international security, Ellen Tauscher, to the chairmen and ranking members of the House and Senate foreign affairs panels. In the letter, Poneman and Tauscher argue that "nuclear trade carries with it a critical nonproliferation

---

[90] Elaine M. Grossman, "U.S. Nuclear Trade Policy Concerns Mounting on Capitol Hill," *Global Security Newswire*, February 17, 2012, http://www.nti.org/gsn/article/us-nuclear-trade-policy-concerns-mounting-capitol-hill/.

advantage in the form of consent rights, along with other opportunities to influence the nuclear policies of our partners. To obtain this advantage, we need to negotiate agreements that our partners can accept and that open doors to U.S. industry." The letter also argues that 123 Agreements are just one of many ways in which the United States can address ENR proliferation concerns.

Inconsistent signals from U.S. political leaders have caused other nations to harbor serious concerns about the reliability of the United States as a nuclear technology provider. For example, news reports following the UAE's decision to purchase South Korean reactor technology hailed the decision as "the right strategic choice" for that country. Nuclear trade and cooperation agreements require a reliable, consistent, and long-term partner, and analysts outside the United States seem to share the view that there are risks in awarding nuclear energy contracts to U.S. firms.

INSUFFICIENT EXPORT INCENTIVES

While the administration's decision not to constrain future nuclear trade negotiations may alleviate one type of export hurdle, other challenges remain. U.S. firms must still compete with firms from other nations on the basis of technological competitiveness, cost, and other factors. While U.S.-based firms still offer some of the most advanced technology available, they do not benefit, as many of their competitors do, from attractive, government-backed export incentives.

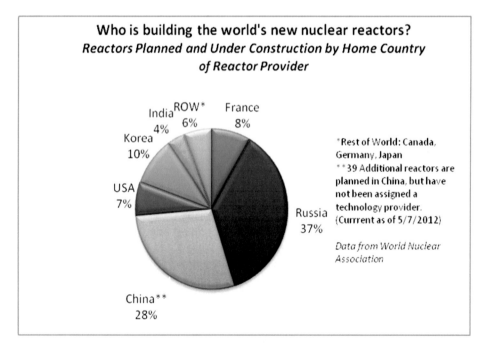

For example, Russian companies—which are currently involved in more than a third of the new reactors currently under construction or planned for construction around the world (see figure above)—often offer turnkey services and fuel take-back programs. This makes them attractive suppliers for countries with limited nuclear infrastructure. And in the South Korea-UAE deal discussed earlier, South Korea's Export-Import Bank expects to lend about $10 billion to Korea

Electric Power Corporation and other contractors to build the four plants the UAE has contracted for.[91]

Of course, not all nuclear power plant construction contracts are even open to competition. Several contracts for reactors under construction in China were awarded to Chinese firms without competition; similarly, the French national utility company did not have to compete for the contract to build a new reactor at Flamanville in France.

The inability to offer generous export incentives, however, puts U.S. firms at a disadvantage for the subset of contracts that is competitively bid worldwide; thus the overall result has been a serious erosion of global market share for U.S. nuclear plant providers. Today, U.S. firms are supplying only 7 percent of the reactors planned or under construction around the world, while Chinese, Russian, Korean, and French firms dominate the global market.

Concern that U.S. nuclear firms are operating at a competitive disadvantage and that this could have longer-term national and global security implications is a central theme of the Poneman/Tauscher letter, which warns that "our competitors are not standing still." The letter goes on to note that "France and Russia in particular are very aggressive in pursuing nuclear business worldwide, and offer favorable terms. Neither imposes ENR conditions in their agreements. Each billion dollars of American nuclear exports supports 10,000 jobs, and provides the U.S. with access and influence over the direction of nuclear programs, ensuring they meet the highest standards for nonproliferation, security, and safety."

For reasons discussed in Chapter 2 of this report, we believe the U.S. has compelling economic and security reasons for maintaining a strong presence in international markets for nuclear energy. This will require continued investment to develop U.S. technology and expertise—particularly in new areas that may hold particular promise for export markets, like small modular reactors (SMRs). It will also require a thoughtful examination of current export policies to explore reforms and improvements that would allow U.S. firms to compete more effectively while still advancing high standards for safety, security, and nonproliferation around the world.

TECHNOLOGICAL COMPETITIVENESS

Today, U.S.-based firms offer several highly competitive nuclear reactor technologies. For example, the Westinghouse AP-1000 design has been embraced by U.S. and Chinese power companies, in part due to its advanced passive safety features (and in part due to its lower estimated cost per megawatt of installed capacity). AP-1000 agreements have been reached with the Czech Republic and Canada and are also under consideration for construction in India and potentially elsewhere.[92]

To maintain or regain a competitive edge in international nuclear markets, U.S. firms will need to continue to offer technology that other nations want to buy. The advanced reactor designs offered for sale today by U.S. firms (such as the AP-1000 and the General Electric/Hitachi-designed

[91] Ayesha Daya, "South Korea Plans to Lend $10 Billion for U.A.E. Nuclear Plants," Bloomberg News, October 7, 2010, http://www.bloomberg.com/news/2010-10-06/south-korea-plans-to-lend-a-total-of-10-billion-for-u-a-e-nuclear-plants.html.
[92] See Westinghouse, News Release, "Westinghouse and Nuclear Power Company of India Limited Sign Memorandum of Understanding for Early Works Agreement," June 13, 2012, http://westinghousenuclear.mediaroom.com/index.php?s=43&item=326; and Westinghouse, News Release, "Westinghouse to Prepare Detailed Construction Plans and Cost Estimates for Potential AP1000 Units at Darlington," July 23, 2012, http://westinghousenuclear.mediaroom.com/index.php?s=43&item=332.

ESBWR) were developed over the course of a decade or more through public-private partnerships such as the DOE's Advanced Light Water Reactor program in the 1990s and the Nuclear Power 2010 program in the 2000s.[93] Given the importance of these successes in terms of broader U.S. trade and security interests, we believe it is appropriate for future technology investments to continue to be supported by both industry and the federal government.

Looking ahead to future markets, it is worth noting that some 60 countries that do not currently have nuclear power plants have approached the IAEA to explore the possibility of acquiring one. The IAEA anticipates that about 15 of these aspiring nuclear nations will proceed to build one or more reactors over the next decade or two.[94] In many of these nations (and in some nations that already have nuclear energy), a large nuclear plant may be poorly suited to local needs. Small modular reactors (SMRs) may offer a better fit for nations with smaller or slower-growing electrical demand. Cooperative public-private efforts are underway in the United States to explore the commercial potential of SMR technology, but the present pace of development may be insufficient to prevent other nations from capturing the lion's share of this potentially important new market.

Meanwhile, ensuring that an array of civilian nuclear technologies (including, but not limited to, SMRs) will be available to meet longer-term energy needs requires keeping the technology R&D pipeline full. Nations like China, India, and others have shown substantial interest in advanced (Generation IV) nuclear reactor and fuel cycle technologies that may be deployed around the middle of the century. This may seem like a long time horizon, but as demonstrated by the time it took to get the AP-1000 and ESBWR designs ready for commercial development, nuclear energy technologies take decades to move through the R&D phases to demonstration and into commercial use. The United States will need to make sustained investments in technology development if it is to maintain a leadership role in commercial nuclear energy.

CHALLENGES IN THE DOMESTIC MARKET

The challenges facing new nuclear plants in the United States come primarily in four areas: cost, waste management, regulation, and public acceptance.

COST

A principal barrier for the U.S. commercial nuclear energy industry is that the construction of new plants cannot, in most U.S. electricity markets today, be justified on the basis of economics alone.

This statement is borne out by the work of the Commission's Financial Structuring Sub-Group. The subgroup analyzed the economics for a single entity proposing to build five new plants total, with staggered construction and start dates. This approach was intended to capture efficiencies and capital cost savings resulting from experience and "learning by doing." Realistically, any entity in the business of building new nuclear power plants is unlikely to plan for just a single reactor; moreover the first new reactor would be expected to cost more and take longer than the fourth or fifth reactor. Other critical assumptions are summarized in the text box.

---

[93] Program information available at Office of Nuclear Energy, http://www.ne.doe.gov/np2010/overview.html.
[94] Blue Ribbon Commission on America's Nuclear Future (BRC), Final Report to the Secretary of Energy, January 2012, p. 110, http://cybercemetery.unt.edu/archive/brc/20120620220235/http://brc.gov/sites/default/files/documents/brc_finalreport_jan2012.pdf.

Key Assumptions in Economic Analysis

- General inflation rate: 2 percent
- Capital structure: 50/50 debt/equity
- Cost of debt: 7 percent (no loan guarantee)
- Overnight capital cost: $6,300/kW ($8.8 billion for first plant)
- Annual escalation on capital costs: 2 percent
- Construction time: 6 years for plants 1 and 2; 5 years for plants 3–5
- Capital cost savings after first plant: 10 percent for each successive plant to a max reduction of 30 percent
- Decommissioning fund: $500 million (2012 $); 8 percent investment return
- Plant capacity: 1,400 MW
- Life of plant: 40 years
- Capacity factor: 93 percent
- Operating statistics (2012 $): Fixed O&M at $10/MWh; fuel at $7.5/MWh; major maintenance at $50/kW-yr
- Power prices: based on Henry Hub natural gas futures through 2024; escalated at 3 percent thereafter
- Capacity prices: blended average of NE and PJM through 2015; escalated at 3 percent thereafter
- Tax rate: 38 percent
- Depreciation: 15-year modified accelerated cost recovery system (MACRS) at time of operation
- Property tax: 1 percent of total cost

It is important to note up front that the assumptions used here are for illustrative purposes only and are intended to represent a middle range of what might be experienced across the United States. The factors included in this list of assumptions may vary greatly from region to region. Thus, our assumptions may differ considerably from the actual conditions facing U.S. companies that have made or are considering making investments in nuclear power.

Projected IRR and NPV: Construction of Five New Nuclear Plants

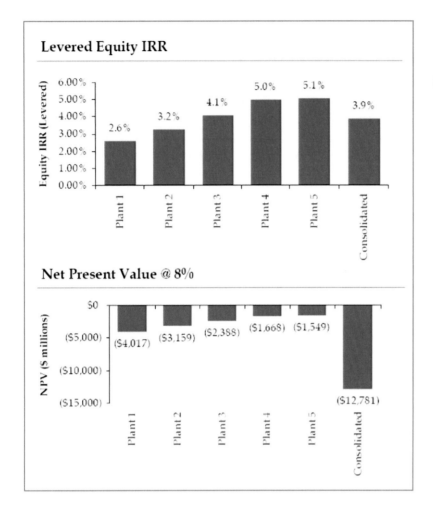

Source: Moelis

For each of the five plants and for all five plants together in our example, we calculated the "levered equity" internal rate of return (IRR) on investment ("levered equity" means that the IRR figures shown include a reduction for debt service payments). The results of the analysis are presented in the figure above and show that, while the reactors in our scenario would produce increasingly positive returns, the returns individually and collectively fall short of the 12–15 percent IRR private investors are typically looking for. In other words, returns under the base case are unattractive and would likely not attract investment. While there is significant improvement through the "learning curve" such that the fifth plant is much more profitable than the first plant (the change in net present value between Plant 1 and Plant 5 is $2.5 billion and the IRR for Plant 5 is nearly double the IRR for Plant 1), the economics are such that even the fifth plant is unlikely to clear the bar for private investment.

Sensitivity Analysis—Low, Middle, and High Plant Construction Costs

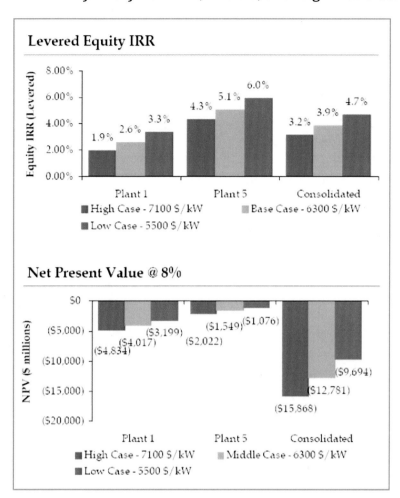

Source: Moelis

In our analysis we assume that construction costs for new nuclear plants in the United States will be high. This is largely due to uncertainties resulting from the decades-long hiatus in nuclear plant construction in this country—a hiatus that has led to the "mummification" of build capabilities and experience. Of course, it is possible that capital costs for a new plant could come in significantly lower (or higher) than assumed in this analysis. To explore this possibility, the Financial Structuring Sub-Group conducted a sensitivity analysis to examine how changes in capital cost would change the attractiveness of new nuclear plant investment. Specifically, the subgroup looked at three overnight capital cost scenarios:

- High: $7,100/kW or $10.0 billion
- Base: $6,300/kW or $8.8 billion
- Low: $5,500/kW or $7.7 billion

The results indicate that even at the low end of the capital cost range considered (i.e., $5,500 per kW), expected returns are still below the levels demanded by most private investors (see figure above).

The finding that new nuclear power plants face steep economic hurdles is not a new one. Concern that these hurdles would effectively preclude private investment in new nuclear plants prompted the inclusion of various construction incentives in the Energy Policy Act of 2005—specifically, federal loan guarantees, production tax credits, and insurance provisions to guard against regulatory delays for new nuclear power plants.

Initially, these provisions—along with a DOE program to provide assistance for new plant licensing and the widespread expectation that Congress would pass some form of regulation to restrict greenhouse gas emissions—succeeded in spurring significant interest in new plants. More than a dozen utilities began licensing activities for new nuclear power plants (see figure below). This resurgence of interest, however, proved relatively short-lived. Today, despite the various incentives in the Energy Policy Act, only two projects seem likely to advance to completion before 2020: the two units being built by Southern Company at its Vogtle site and two units proposed by Scana Corporation for the V.C. Summer site.

New Nuclear Plant License Applications

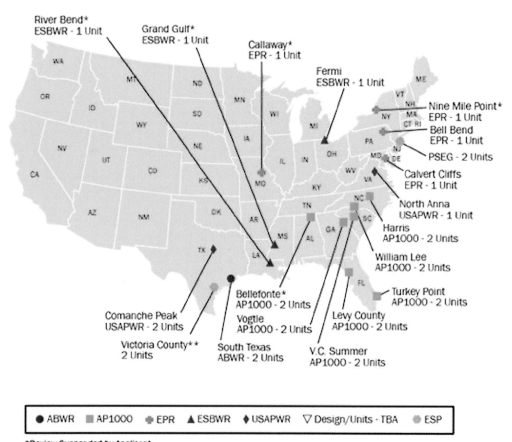

*Review Suspended by Applicant
** COL Application Amended by Applicant to ESP on 03/25/2010

There are several reasons why the momentum behind new plant construction has waned. To be sure, the inability of the federal government and utility applicants to agree on loan guarantee terms is high on the list (today, nearly seven years after the loan guarantee program was codified, not a single loan guarantee for a nuclear power plant has been finalized). The failure of the federal incentive programs notwithstanding, no factor has dampened enthusiasm for new nuclear as much as the radically altered supply and price outlook for natural gas.

Natural gas prices, which averaged as high as $8 per million BTU in 2008, now average about $4. EIA predicts prices will remain below $5 by 2018[95] [see figure below] despite increasing demand—particularly in the electricity sector, where the U.S. Energy Information Administration (EIA) shows that natural gas consumption grew by 21 percent in 2012.[96]

The expectation that natural gas prices will remain relatively low and stable, despite increasing demand, reflects an assumption that domestic natural gas production will continue to grow. In fact, EIA projections indicate that the United States will become a net exporter of liquefied natural gas starting in 2016, and will be an overall net exporter of natural gas by 2021.[97]

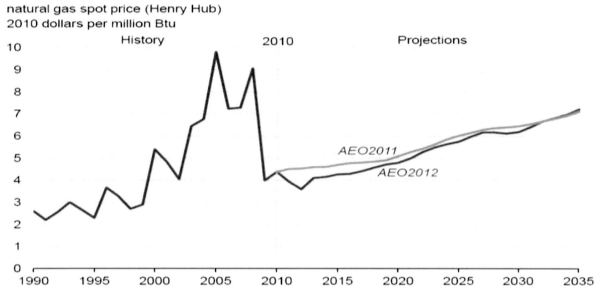

natural gas spot price (Henry Hub)
2010 dollars per million Btu

Sources: EIA, Annual Energy Outlook 2012 Early Release and EIA, Annual Energy Outlook 2011

In an environment where electricity prices are driven by the availability of low-cost and abundant natural gas, new nuclear cannot compete on the basis of economic factors alone, particularly so long as greenhouse gas emissions remain unrestricted (and unpriced). While the importance of the two new reactor projects underway in the United States should not be underestimated, it is now clear that the federal incentives included in the Energy Policy Act of 2005 will not be sufficient to spur a new wave of utility investment in nuclear technology. As growing numbers of existing plants retire, different and/or more generous forms of support will be needed to sustain a meaningful role for nuclear power in the U.S. electricity generating mix going forward.

As discussed in Chapter 1, a critical enabling factor for the two new plants that are moving forward at this time (Vogtle and Summer) is support from state regulators that helps reduce the stress on cash flow and earnings during the construction period. Specifically, public utility commissions in Georgia, South Carolina, and a handful of other states have provided the rate

[95] U.S. Energy Information Administration, "Annual Energy Outlook 2012 Early Release," January 23, 2012, http://www.eia.gov/todayinenergy/detail.cfm?id=4671#.
[96] U.S. Energy Information Administration, "Short-Term Energy Outlook," March 6, 2012, http://www.eia.gov/forecasts/steo/archives/mar12.pdf.
[97] U.S. Energy Information Administration, "Annual Energy Outlook 2012 Early Release."

treatment needed to support investment in new plants,[98] at least in part because the addition of new nuclear capacity is consistent with their integrated resource planning processes, which typically allow for the consideration of factors such as stability and diversity of long-term electricity supply. But in providing favorable rate treatment, utility commissions are shifting a portion of the risks and liabilities of nuclear plant investments to ratepayers.[99] Even where there is state-level support for these investments now, the political environment could change, particularly if the new reactors presently under construction experience the types of cost overruns and schedule delays that plagued nuclear plants constructed in the United States in the 1970s and 1980s.

For merchant owners/operators, the risks are even greater, and credit rating agencies and shareholders are even less likely to support a sustained campaign of investment in a new generation of nuclear plants. This is especially obvious when one considers the market capitalization of even the largest merchant owners/operators in comparison to the cost of a single nuclear reactor, let alone multiple units. As discussed in Chapter 1, even the largest of the privately held companies that supply most of the electricity in the United States has a market capitalization of less than $40 billion (and most have a market cap of less than $20 billion). Additionally, merchant markets do not provide a mechanism to fully value factors like reliability, clean air compliance value, fuel diversity, and price stability that may argue in favor of new nuclear investments; these markets are inherently focused on the short term. But in any case, whether a company is operating in regulated or competitive markets, the decision to invest up to $10 billion or more in a new nuclear power plant is one that won't be taken lightly. Under current market conditions, this decision is unlikely to be taken at all.

For new nuclear energy projects to go forward, the national interest and common good objectives and benefits discussed in Chapter 2 need to be recognized, and the federal government and states need to bring policy alternatives to the table. When new projects are "in the money," these national interest and common good benefits will be realized by the market without any direct financial cost to the government. But when the economics of new nuclear plants are "out of the money," private investors and shareholders will not proceed absent government incentives or subsidies that reflect these public interest considerations.

WASTE MANAGEMENT

Finding a long-term solution to the problem of spent nuclear fuel has long been viewed as a challenge that must be met if nuclear power is going to remain viable. At present, several states (California, Connecticut, Illinois, Kentucky, Maine, New Jersey, Oregon, West Virginia, and Wisconsin) prohibit new nuclear plant construction until certain waste management conditions are met.[100] There have been several attempts to repeal these laws in recent years, but none have been successful to date.[101]

More recently, challenges to the NRC's so-called "waste confidence" decisions have brought heightened attention to the nuclear waste issue. The first waste confidence decision was issued in

---

[98] Sony Ben-Moshe et al., "Financing the Nuclear Renaissance: The Benefits and Potential Pitfalls of Federal & State Government Subsidies and the Future of Nuclear Power in California," *Energy Law Journal*, Vol. 30:497, 2009, p. 497.
[99] Ibid.
[100] Blue Ribbon Commission on America's Nuclear Future (BRC), Final Report to the Secretary of Energy, January 2012, p. 25.
[101] Ibid.

1984; more recently, in 2010, the NRC issued a revised decision. In it, the NRC expressed confidence that spent nuclear fuel can be safely stored at U.S. nuclear power plants for at least 60 years beyond the licensed life of the plant; the NRC also expressed confidence that sufficient disposal capacity will be available when needed.[102]

Despite that confidence, the Obama administration's decision in January 2010 to withdraw the Yucca Mountain license application has clearly complicated the nuclear waste picture. Four states appealed the NRC's recent waste confidence statement in light of the decision to terminate the Yucca Mountain project, and in June 2012, the U.S. Court of Appeals directed the NRC to conduct a more thorough environmental analysis before issuing a revised decision on waste confidence.[103] The Commonwealth of Massachusetts is now using this court decision as a basis to challenge the NRC's decision to grant a 20-year extension of the operating license for the Pilgrim nuclear power plant.[104]

Following his decision to withdraw the license application for Yucca Mountain, President Obama directed the secretary of energy to form a Blue Ribbon Commission on America's Nuclear Future to recommend a new strategy for nuclear waste management in the United States. The report subsequently issued by the Blue Ribbon Commission (BRC) in January 2012 concluded: "this nation's failure to come to grips with the nuclear waste issue has already proved damaging and costly and it will be more damaging and more costly the longer it continues: damaging to prospects for maintaining a potentially important energy supply option for the future, damaging to state–federal relations and public confidence in the federal government's competence, and damaging to America's standing in the world—not only as a source of nuclear technology and policy expertise but as a leader on global issues of nuclear safety, non-proliferation, and security."[105]

The Commission's recommended strategy for resolving the nation's nuclear waste impasse included eight key elements:

1. A new, consent-based approach to siting future nuclear waste management facilities.
2. A new organization dedicated solely to implementing the waste management program and empowered with the authority and resources to succeed.
3. Access to the funds nuclear utility ratepayers are providing for the purpose of nuclear waste management.
4. Prompt efforts to develop one or more geologic disposal facilities.
5. Prompt efforts to develop one or more consolidated storage facilities.
6. Prompt efforts to prepare for the eventual large-scale transport of spent nuclear fuel and high-level waste to consolidated storage and disposal facilities when such facilities become available.
7. Support for continued U.S. innovation in nuclear energy technology and for workforce development.

[102] Ibid., p. 26.
[103] World Nuclear News, "Court rejects NRC used fuel ruling," June 11, 2012, http://www.world-nuclear-news.org/WR-Court_rejects_NRC_used_fuel_ruling-1106124.html.
[104] World Nuclear News, "NRC Reactor Licensing Decisions Challenged," June 20, 2012, http://www.world-nuclear-news.org/RS-NRC_reactor_licensing_decisions_challenged-2006124.html.
[105] Blue Ribbon Commission on America's Nuclear Future (BRC), Final Report to the Secretary of Energy, January 2012, p. vi.

8.   Active U.S. leadership in international efforts to address safety, waste management, nonproliferation, and security concerns.[106]

In response to the BRC final report, the Department of Energy (DOE) published an implementation plan titled "Strategy for the Management and Disposal of Used Nuclear Fuel and High-level Radioactive Waste" in January 2013. The strategy proposed a management system composed of the following:

- A pilot, interim storage facility with limited capacity that will be focused on spent fuel from decommissioned plant sites to be opened by 2021;
- A larger, consolidated storage facility to be open by 2025; and
- A permanent geologic repository for the disposal of used nuclear fuel and high-level radioactive waste to be opened in 2048.

The strategy also calls for the establishment of a new, used-fuel management entity outside of DOE with assured access to long-term, stable funding. The strategy endorses a consent-based siting approach for both the consolidated storage facilities and a geologic repository. The strategy also presumes that the Yucca Mountain site will not be used. DOE outlined their current activities in used fuel space at the end of the document, including transportation infrastructure and planning and disposal-related research.

A key message in the DOE strategy is that the Department needs congressional direction before implementing the planned system of storage and disposal facilities.

Adoption of the BRC's recommendations would go a long way toward restoring confidence that the federal government is serious about meeting its waste management commitments and would lower one of the barriers to the construction of new nuclear power plants in the United States.

REGULATORY UNCERTAINTY AND UNPREDICTABILITY

U.S. nuclear plant operators face a greater regulatory burden than operators in any other nation. While the regulatory system in the United States has provided a model for other nations and has been effective in ensuring safe operation of the U.S. reactor fleet, there is concern that regulations have continued to expand without adequate consideration of costs and benefits.

We believe it is essential that the NRC and the U.S. nuclear industry work constructively to maintain the safety and security of the U.S. nuclear fleet without placing undue burdens on reactor operators. As we noted in Chapter 1, the U.S. commercial industry has been unrelenting in its quest for excellence. The Institute of Nuclear Power Operations (INPO) has been a strong force for self-regulation and the result has been performance that sets the global standard. According to nuclear industry reports, however, capital expenditures for regulatory compliance have tripled over just the past five years. Added regulatory requirements when they produce real benefits are good for the industry; additional regulatory costs without appropriate benefits will weigh down otherwise well-performing nuclear facilities and their staff, and will contribute to financial pressures that could lead to even more rapid shutdowns of presently operating nuclear power plants.

---

[106] Ibid., p. vii.

PUBLIC AND POLITICAL SUPPORT

Favorability ratings continue an upward trend, buoyed by high public ratings for safety at America's reactors (7 out of 10 give them high safety marks). By February 2013, support had risen to 68 percent. The industry saw a temporary downturn in public support after the Fukushima accident, falling to a low of 46 percent in April 2011—just after the accident. Seventy-three percent of respondents now believe that nuclear plants operating in the United States are safe and secure, with 24 percent thinking they are not. Also, 65 percent believe that "nuclear power plants in this area are able to withstand the most extreme natural events that may occur here."[107]

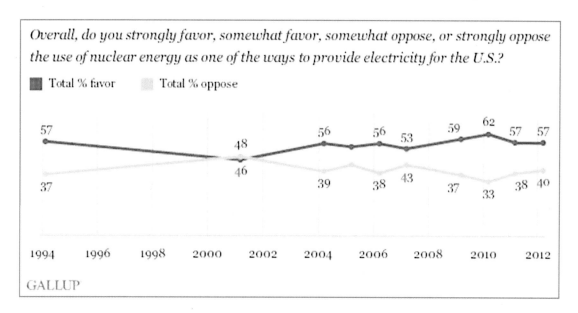

Overall, do you strongly favor, somewhat favor, somewhat oppose, or strongly oppose the use of nuclear energy as one of the ways to provide electricity for the U.S.?

At the federal level, nuclear power has generally enjoyed bipartisan political support; in recent years, successive administrations and Congress have backed continued funding for nuclear energy R&D along with a variety of incentives and subsidies aimed at kick-starting the domestic industry. As noted earlier, however, policies adopted as part of the Energy Policy Act of 2005 have yet to stimulate construction commitments beyond the units currently planned for the Vogtle and Summer sites. The federal loan guarantee program, in particular, has not worked as intended, while the other two incentive programs in the Act—the production tax credit and insurance to guard against regulatory delays—cannot be used until new plants are operating or at least under construction.

The primary problem involves the credit subsidy cost—the fee charged to project developers for the loan guarantee. Credit subsidy costs for the Department of Energy's loan guarantee program are calculated using a credit subsidy calculator developed by the Office of Management and Budget. Of the major inputs to the calculator, two of them—default probability and recovery rate in the event of default—have the greatest impact on results. The Executive Branch employs a recovery rate of 55 percent across the board for all energy technologies and projects being considered for Title XVII loan guarantees. This assumption inflates the credit subsidy cost well

---

[107] Nuclear Energy Institute, News Release, "New Poll Shows Americans' Support for Nuclear Energy, New Facilities Remains Solid," Bisconti Research, Inc. with GfK Roper survey, February 11, 2013, http://www.nei.org/newsandevents/newsreleases/New-Poll-Shows-Americans%E2%80%99-Support-for-Nuclear-Ener.

beyond the level required to compensate the federal government for the risk taken in providing the loan guarantee. At least one nuclear power project was quoted an unrealistically high credit subsidy cost, which ignored the project's strong credit metrics and the robust lender protections built into the transaction. The 55-percent recovery rate now used is well below the recovery rates historically observed for regulated utility debt and project finance debt. According to historical data, recovery rates for these types of debt typically range from approximately 85 percent to 100 percent.

It is vitally important that credit subsidy costs be calculated accurately. If current practices continue, the Executive Branch will continue to produce inflated credit subsidy costs. Project sponsors, in turn, will simply abandon otherwise creditworthy nuclear energy projects, and the nation will forego the carbon-free energy and thousands of well-paying jobs represented by these facilities.

Going forward, severe budget pressures and an overall climate of fiscal austerity, coupled with diminished public enthusiasm for nuclear energy in the aftermath of Fukushima, are likely to further constrain the federal government's capacity and willingness to provide financial incentives for new plant construction.

At the state level, there is greater variation in the degree of political and policy support for nuclear energy. As noted earlier, several states have adopted moratoriums on new plant construction until issues such as waste management are addressed. At the other end of the spectrum, at least a handful of states have adopted policies aimed at promoting investment in new reactors, in some cases by supplementing financial incentives provided by the federal government.

In states with rate-regulated utilities, the most commonly used policy lever to encourage nuclear construction involves favorable rate treatment that allows utilities to recover the capital costs of new plants. Typically, utilities are allowed to include construction costs in their rate-base. In this way, utilities are assured of being able to recover their costs, in some cases even before construction is complete and the plant has begun to operate. In states that do not permit utilities to recover costs during plant construction, the public utility commission typically approves costs on a non-appealable, year-to-year basis. Approved costs are included in the rate-base and can begin to be recovered upon commercial operation or abandonment. And both rate-regulated states and states that have restructured their electricity markets provide tax credits or exemptions for new nuclear construction. For example, Kansas exempts new nuclear facilities from state property taxes, while Texas permits school districts to enter into agreements with developers of new nuclear plants to limit the appraised value of the plants for purposes of assessing property taxes for school district maintenance and operations.[108]

Many of these state-level incentives were put in place in the mid-to-late 2000s, when the prospects for new nuclear power plant construction looked quite positive. Today, in the aftermath of the Fukushima accident, there is less state-level support for the construction of new nuclear power plants. For example, efforts by the Minnesota House and Senate to lift a statewide ban on building new nuclear power plants stalled in 2011 following the Fukushima accident.[109] In Indiana, an

---

[108] Sony Ben-Moshe et al., "Financing the Nuclear Renaissance: The Benefits and Potential Pitfalls of Federal & State Government Subsidies and the Future of Nuclear Power in California," *Energy Law Journal*, Vol. 30:497, 2009.
[109] Tim Pugmire, "Plan to repeal Minn. ban on new nuclear power on hold," Minnesota Public Radio, March 14, 2011, http://minnesota.publicradio.org/display/web/2011/03/14/minnesota-nuclear-ban-repeal-on-hold.

initiative that would have provided incentives for companies to invest in clean energy, including nuclear power, passed the state senate but did not advance further because of events in Japan.[110]

ERODED SUPPLY CHAIN AND AGING WORKFORCE

From the earliest stages of development, the successful construction of new nuclear plants depends on a robust supply chain of nuclear equipment manufacturers. Because nuclear plants are made up of hundreds of specialized components and subcomponents, the industry requires a deep and diverse supplier base.

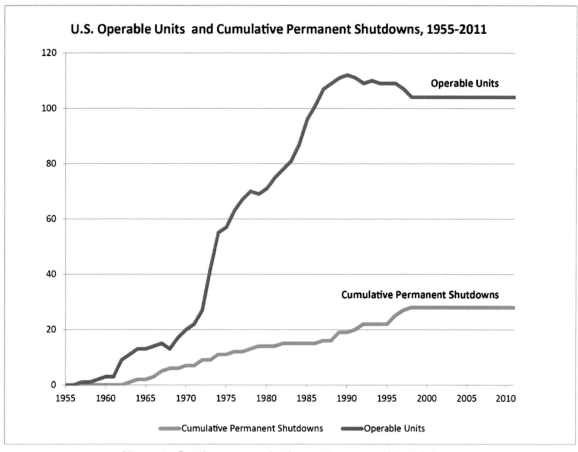

Source: EIA

*Does not reflect the two recent shutdowns at Kewaunee and Crystal River

From the early 1970s to the late 1980s, the United States was engaged in a vigorous program of new nuclear power plant construction.[111] As seen in the figure above, about 100 nuclear power reactors were completed in the United States during that period.

These plants were built according to U.S.-developed designs; they included major components (such as reactor pressure vessels, steam generators, and pumps) that were built in the United States, and they operated on uranium that was enriched at the U.S. government's enrichment

---

[110] John Russell, "Indiana's interest in nuclear power is dampened," Indystar.com, March 17, 2011, http://www.indystar.com/article/20110317/LOCAL/103170407/Indiana-s-interest-nuclear-power-dampened.
[111] American Council on Global Nuclear Competitiveness (ACGNC), "The U.S. Domestic Civil Nuclear Infrastructure and U.S. Nonproliferation Policy," May 2007, p. 15.

plants and fabricated into fuel assemblies at facilities operated by companies like General Electric, Westinghouse, and Exxon Nuclear.

Today, however, these U.S.-based capabilities have atrophied. According to a 2005 assessment[112] of the state of the infrastructure for building new nuclear power plants, "major equipment (reactor pressure vessels, steam generators and moisture separator reheaters) for the near-term deployment of [new] units would not be manufactured by United States facilities" and that "reactor pressure vessel (RPV) fabrication could be delayed by the limited availability of the large nuclear-grade forgings that are currently only available from one Japanese supplier."

The 2005 report concluded that "the necessary manufacturing, fabrication, labor, and construction equipment infrastructure is available today or can be readily developed to support the construction and commissioning of up to eight nuclear units during the period from 2010 to 2017." The ability of U.S. manufacturers to support the construction of eight new nuclear power reactors in an eight-year period stands in sharp contrast to the U.S. industry's previous ability to support construction of 30–40 nuclear plants in a similar timeframe.[113]

Another important development has been the acquisition of all but one American firm engaged in light-water reactor and nuclear-fuel design and manufacture by a non-U.S.-based competitor. As we noted in Chapter 1, Westinghouse—creator of the AP-1000—was purchased by Toshiba in 2006 (Toshiba purchased Westinghouse from British Nuclear Fuels, Ltd., which had acquired Westinghouse from CBS in 1996).[114] Even the sole remaining U.S. vendor of commercial nuclear power plants—the General Electric Company—has partnered with the Japanese companies Hitachi and Toshiba to form Global Nuclear Fuel; GE retains 51 percent ownership, while Hitachi and Toshiba hold the balance.[115]

Besides the loss of U.S.-based manufacturing and design capability at the firm level, workforce adequacy is a significant challenge for the domestic nuclear industry going forward. Large numbers of skilled design engineers, construction specialists, and operating staff are needed to successfully design, build, and eventually operate a new generation of reactors. The U.S. industry has been working diligently for the past five years to reinforce and streamline processes from their four main workforce sources: labor organizations, community colleges, universities, and the military.

This effort was needed independent of new nuclear construction since a large portion of the current nuclear workforce is reaching retirement age. These workforce pipelines are needed to ensure there is qualified staff available to keep existing plants operating.

Jobs in the nuclear energy industry require a high degree of skill. Given the decades-long hiatus in new nuclear plant builds (prior to Vogtle, the last plant to start construction was Palo Verde, in 1979), the industry did not seem to offer a bright career path and, not surprisingly, the number of young people interested in acquiring these skills dwindled. With enrollment declining,

---

[112] MPR Associates, Inc., "DOE NP2010 Nuclear Power Plant Construction Infrastructure Assessment," MPR-2776, Rev. 0, October 21, 2005.

[113] American Council on Global Nuclear Competiveness, "The U.S. Domestic Civil Nuclear Infrastructure," p. 15.
[114] *Pittsburgh Business Times*, "Westinghouse sold to Toshiba for $5.4B," February 6, 2006, http://www.bizjournals.com/pittsburgh/stories/2006/02/06/daily3.html.
[115] American Council on Global Nuclear Competiveness, "The U.S. Domestic Civil Nuclear Infrastructure," p. 16.

universities and technical schools closed their nuclear engineering and related skills-based programs.

While the energy sector generally needs more science professionals, the nuclear energy industry faces a particularly worrisome demographic shift, according to recent reports by the Center for Energy Workforce Development. A 2011 study by the Nuclear Energy Institute (NEI) echoed this conclusion; it found that approximately 39 percent of the current nuclear utility workforce will be eligible to retire in the next five years. The report also found that "general attrition"—that is, people simply changing jobs—will reduce the workforce by an additional 10 percent.[116] The combination of expected retirements and attrition amounts to about 25,000 job vacancies that would need to be filled by the nuclear energy industry by 2016.

The industry has responded to this phenomenon by acting collectively to address workforce development, so that workers at all levels can succeed in nuclear energy jobs. Beginning in 2007, the industry began to reinforce the four main workforce pipelines into the nuclear energy industry. Universities, community colleges, labor organizations, and the military are the main pathways into commercial nuclear energy careers.

Separate and distinct strategies were initiated to ensure these pipelines were functional. These strategies have been successful. The universities with nuclear engineering programs have seen a steady increase in enrollments. Community colleges with nuclear technology programs have been reestablished and have grown from 4 to 37 since 2007. The Building and Construction Trades Department of the AFL-CIO has established training centers and new apprenticeship programs to support nuclear energy careers, and the U.S. Navy has just implemented a first-of-its-kind program that streamlines recruiting efforts for the nuclear energy industry by providing the contact information of all of their separating navy nukes who want to pursue civilian nuclear careers.

Of course, the need for technically trained workers is not confined to the nuclear field. A 2008 study by Tapping America's Potential, a coalition representing a diverse group of high-tech and industrial employers, estimates that by 2015, the country will need to graduate roughly 400,000 students per year with degrees in science, technology, engineering, and math (STEM) to meet overall high-tech workforce demands.[117] In 2006, the number of STEM graduates was 225,660[118]— just a little more than half the number needed to meet the nation's needs a few short years from now.

In addition to increasing throughput of Americans in STEM education programs, broader efforts are underway to increase women and minority graduation from STEM programs. This is because both women and minorities hold a disproportionately low share of STEM degrees.[119] Women make up 50 percent of the population, but only 20 percent of engineering school graduates are women.[120] Although African Americans make up 12 percent of the population, they received just 7

---

[116] Nuclear Energy Institute, "Help Wanted: 25,000 Skilled Workers for the Nuclear Energy Industry," Summer 2011, http://www.nei.org/resourcesandstats/publicationsandmedia/insight/insight-web-extra/help-wanted-25000-skilled-workers.
[117] Tapping America's Potential: The Education for Innovation Initiative, "Gaining Momentum, Losing Ground," 2008 Progress Report, http://tapcoalition.org/resource/pdf/tap_2008_progress.pdf.
[118] Ibid., p. 3.
[119] U.S. Department of Commerce, "Women in STEM: A Gender Gap to Innovation," August 2011, http://www.esa.doc.gov/sites/default/files/reports/documents/womeninstemagaptoinnovation8311.pdf.
[120] Nadya Fouad and Romila Singh, "Stemming the Tide: Why Women Leave Engineering," University of Wisconsin-Milwaukee, 2011, http://studyofwork.com/files/2011/03/NSF_Women-Full-Report-0314.pdf.

percent of all STEM bachelor's degrees, 4 percent of master's degrees, and two percent of PhD degrees in 2009.[121]

The nuclear energy industry wishes to have the best available workforce for both the operating units and any new units that U.S. firms support. Continuing to support workforce development programs while improving company-specific training programs will continue to be a challenge during the transition from the baby boomer to the millennial generation.

In the next part of this report we turn to a "toolkit" of options for policymakers and the industry to address the challenges described in this chapter.

---

[121] U.S. Department of Education, National Center for Education Statistics, "Students Who Study Science, Technology, Engineering, and Mathematics (STEM) in Postsecondary Education," NCES 2009-161, July 2009, http://nces.ed.gov/pubs2009/2009161.pdf.

Chapter 4

RECOMMENDATIONS

This chapter recommends specific actions to ensure (a) that nuclear energy remains available as a viable energy option for the United States and (b) that the U.S. government retains a position of strong influence in international nuclear energy matters. Success in both of these objectives would advance U.S. security interests and deliver environmental and energy diversity benefits for the American people beyond those recognized in the marketplace. It therefore warrants support beyond what the market—left to private considerations of risk and reward alone—will provide.

As discussed in Chapter 3, a large number of new domestic nuclear power plant orders is highly unlikely over at least the next several years owing to many factors, particularly low natural gas prices. So while we believe the federal government and state governments should take steps to facilitate future plant orders, the focus of our recommendations is on the return of U.S. competitiveness in the trade of nuclear technology and equipment. Restored U.S. competitiveness will enhance U.S. influence in international nuclear affairs. Conversely, if U.S. firms are unable to compete in the global marketplace, the lack of a competitive U.S. presence in commercial markets, coupled with a diminishing role for nuclear energy in U.S. electricity generation, will mean the United States will not be able to project its interests in civil nuclear matters and nonproliferation as forcefully.[122]

Of course, there is no single policy step the government can take to restore the strength of the U.S. nuclear industry. And government cannot do it all—industry will still need to develop attractive technology offerings and deliver a quality product or service consistent with the cost and schedule requirements of their customers. The goal of a new U.S. nuclear energy program should therefore be multifaceted. It should facilitate trade opportunities for U.S companies; it should address the barriers and challenges that are inhibiting development of existing domestic projects; it should address opportunities for developing new technologies and intellectual capital; and it should provide a strong basis for extending U.S. influence to shape the global nuclear energy infrastructure as it evolves in the decades ahead. In this chapter, we offer a range of policy actions that can move us toward this goal.

DEVELOPING POLICY SOLUTIONS THAT MEET THE NEEDS OF INDUSTRY AND GOVERNMENT

In designing options for addressing the challenges to a robust commercial nuclear enterprise, and in light of the foregoing discussion, we have striven to evaluate only those policy options that would be most consistent with the needs and objectives of the federal government, state governments, and the private sector.

NEEDS AND OBJECTIVES OF THE FEDERAL GOVERNMENT

- Arresting the decline of U.S. influence in nonproliferation policy and nuclear energy standard setting. With a nearly dormant domestic nuclear energy industry and other countries (China, Russia, South Korea, India) taking leading roles in an expanding global market, the U.S. government is finding it challenging to maintain important policy

---

[122] American Council on Global Nuclear Competiveness, "The U.S. Domestic Civil Nuclear Infrastructure," p. 27–28.

directions related to all dimensions of nuclear energy. Nonproliferation, trade guidelines, standards for operation, approaches for emergency response are all areas where the United States needs to continue to exert global leadership.

- Confronting a challenging fiscal climate. With so many financial demands, and in a challenging economic environment, providing federal or state incentives or other financial support is difficult. Lawmakers should seek a long-term "budget neutral" level of support, or as close to budget neutral as reasonable, while supporting "program" success. Policies should be designed to ensure that incentives "sunset" or otherwise phase down as conditions for new nuclear improve.
- Overcoming recent controversies with DOE programs, including the loan guarantee program. DOE credibility and the controversy surrounding recent loan guarantee awards is a barrier to progress with the federal nuclear program in its current form. This will only increase the bureaucratic inertia and aversion to informed risk-taking that has stalled and frustrated the implementation of existing incentive programs. At the same time, these programs must be designed to minimize opportunities for waste, fraud, and abuse.
- Encouraging and incentivizing broad risk-taking and investment by the private sector and investor entities so as to minimize federal project risk exposure. The desire to minimize taxpayer exposure will multiply in light of the Solyndra default and other negative publicity associated with the existing DOE loan guarantee program.

NEEDS AND OBJECTIVES OF STATE GOVERNMENTS

- Creating job opportunities and other economic benefits. State and local governments are keenly aware of the need to spur job growth as a way to increase tax revenues and reduce demand for unemployment and other social "safety net" benefits.
- Attracting manufacturing and service company expansion. To the extent that local companies can provide supplies and services for new nuclear power plants in the United States and abroad, state-level political support will be even stronger.
- Maintaining reliable, diversified, and reasonably priced electricity supply. States may be simultaneously attracted by the stable generating costs and alarmed by the high construction price tag and historical cost over-runs associated with nuclear power. State public utility commissions will tend to value the price stability that can come with a diversified electricity supply.

NEEDS AND OBJECTIVES OF THE PRIVATE SECTOR

- Reasonable financial returns. Both the suppliers and buyers of nuclear power plant technology will need assurance that the export of nuclear technologies and services abroad and the construction of new reactors in the United States (as well as the continued operation of existing reactors) can provide financial returns commensurate with their risk.
- Consistent government support for nuclear energy. Wide swings in federal and state government support for nuclear energy will dampen private-sector enthusiasm for investing in the nuclear business.
- Limited financial risks. The level of investment required to construct a new plant should be reduced to the extent possible and, ideally, these investments will receive favorable treatment (such as through tax benefits or inclusion in electric rates).
- Opportunity to maintain a diversified portfolio of electricity supply sources. Electricity generating companies would be more inclined to maintain a diverse generating portfolio

if they were compensated for the societal benefits associated with maintaining a diversified portfolio.

- Variety of solutions so as to address the variety of economic energy environments across the nation (strongly regulated areas, areas with lighter regulation, semi-open competitive markets, and fully competitive market areas). Every electricity generator faces a unique set of regulatory and legislative circumstances; the menu of policy solutions should reflect this reality and allow for the tailoring of incentives.

Based on the analysis in earlier sections of this report and the considerations enumerated above, we have concluded that the following policy options are most likely to be effective in reinvigorating the domestic nuclear energy enterprise.

BOLSTERING U.S. COMPETITIVENESS IN EXPORT MARKETS

As discussed in Chapter 3, U.S. national security interests can be served effectively only if U.S. suppliers of nuclear technology, fuel, and services play an active role in the global marketplace. At present, the ability of U.S. firms to compete in this marketplace is severely hindered by U.S. export policies. Over the longer term, the United States may find itself at a further disadvantage if its nuclear technology offerings fall behind those of other nuclear exporters.

Improving the ability of U.S. firms to compete in the global nuclear marketplace is our highest-priority recommendation. Our reasoning is straightforward. A large-scale, government-supported nuclear construction program in the United States would be cost-prohibitive. On the other hand, there are several other nations that have placed a higher priority on the nonmonetary advantages of nuclear energy and are therefore aggressively investing in new reactors. Rather than rest our hopes primarily on an expensive program of domestic industry supports, we believe that recommendations focused on making it easier for U.S. firms to compete in the international marketplace have a greater likelihood of being implemented and a greater chance of achieving our goals.

Consistent with this objective, we view as positive the administration's recent acknowledgment that most nations will not be willing to give up their NPT rights to enrichment and reprocessing technology, and we support the decision to avoid insisting on the so-called "gold standard" in pending 123 Agreements, such as those with Vietnam and Jordan. The administration's plan to adopt a "case-by-case" policy to negotiating future agreements recognizes that in order to benefit from the nonproliferation advantages that come from nuclear trade, the United States must "negotiate agreements that our partners can accept."[123]

The administration's recognition of the realities of the international nuclear marketplace is certainly welcome but is not sufficient to bolster the competitiveness of U.S. firms. We can and must do more. In particular, the combination of export barriers, insufficient export incentives available to U.S. firms, and the noncompetitive nature of some contract awards, have led to a serious erosion of market share for U.S. nuclear plant providers such that U.S. firms are supplying only a small share (6 percent) of the reactors planned or under construction across the globe, while Chinese, Russian, Korean, and French firms dominate the global market.

---

[123] Letter from Daniel B. Poneman and Ellen O. Tauscher to Senator John Kerry, Chairman, Committee of Foreign Relations, January 10, 2012.

To help restore the competitiveness of U.S. nuclear energy technology exports, we recommend adoption of the following policies:

- 123 Agreements: The negotiation of future 123 Agreements on a case-by-case basis—rather than insisting that nations cede their NPT rights to nuclear fuel cycle technologies—is the approach most likely to support U.S. nuclear exports. This policy should be the norm and should be recognized as such by the U.S. Congress.
- Part 810 Requirements: Part 810 prohibits U.S. companies from assisting foreign nuclear power programs unless such assistance is authorized by the secretary of energy, following an interagency review process specified by the Atomic Energy Act. These requirements can stand in the way of U.S. nuclear companies' ability to conduct routine business. The current Part 810 rules are already restrictive, but changes proposed by DOE staff in 2011 would only make matters worse. In any revision of the Section 810 rules, efforts should be made to take into full account the concerns raised by U.S. nuclear firms.
- Government Support for Exports and Export Financing: The federal government should issue a clear policy statement in support of nuclear technology exports, should ensure that this policy is implemented consistently by the relevant federal agencies, and should undertake a concerted effort to streamline the cumbersome export approval process. In particular, U.S. exports would be aided by favorable interest rates enabled by loans from the Export-Import Bank of the United States, which was formed for the purposes of financing and insuring foreign purchases of U.S. goods for customers unable or unwilling to accept credit risk. The Ex-Im Bank "assume[s] credit and country risks that the private sector is unable or unwilling to accept." It also "help[s] to level the playing field for U.S. exporters by matching the financing that other governments provide to their exporters."[124]

EXPANDED SUPPORT FOR SMRs AND TECHNOLOGY DEVELOPMENT

To regain a competitive edge in international nuclear markets, U.S. firms will need to offer technology that other nations want to buy. Small modular reactors (SMRs), leading versions of which are under development by U.S. firms, may offer a better fit for nations with smaller or slower-growing electrical demand. As discussed in Chapter 3, cooperative public-private efforts are underway in the United States to explore the commercial potential of SMR technology. Specifically, DOE is engaged in a multiyear program (known as the SMR Licensing Technical Support Program) to help accelerate the timeline for commercializing and deploying SMR technologies. The mission of the program is to overcome first-of-its-kind cost hurdles associated with design certification and licensing activities for two SMR designs through cost-share arrangements with industry partners. DOE has requested a budget of $65 million to continue the program in fiscal year 2013.[125]

Despite this welcome DOE support, there are of course no guarantees that industry will proceed with the construction of SMRs in the United States. To improve prospects for deployment, one option is to allow the Department of Defense (DOD) to participate directly in funding the development and demonstration of SMRs, perhaps through DOE, with the project meeting civil nuclear requirements for licensing and regulation. In recent years, DOD has investigated the

[124] Export-Import Bank of the United States, Mission Statement, http://www.exim.gov/about/library/reports/annualreports/2010/upload/exim_2010annualreport_mission.pdf.
[125] U.S. Department of Energy, "FY 2013 Congressional Budget Request," Volume 3, February 2012, p. 299, http://energy.gov/sites/prod/files/FY13%20DOE%20Congressional%20Budget%20Request%20-%20Volume3.pdf.

potential application of SMRs to provide electricity to deployed troops and to reduce reliance on the domestic electrical grid.[126] A DOE/DOD SMR development and demonstration program would not only create domestic opportunities, it would also provide a pathway for U.S. firms to demonstrate the readiness of SMR technology for deployment overseas.

Meanwhile, DOE's SMR development efforts should be continued and expanded, as envisioned under DOE's current program plans. Going forward, these plans should allow for the parallel development of materials, fabrication, manufacturing, assembly, and operation of SMRs by several different vendors. The idea would be to meet NRC licensing requirements while maintaining flexibility to innovate and iterate throughout the development process.

Assuming success in these development efforts, SMR vendors should be encouraged to pursue global market opportunities while also advancing the highest U.S. standards for safety, security, reliability, and emergency response as applicable to this new technology. The same economic and financial structuring incentives available for light-water reactors should also be made available for SMRs. Commercialization should be accompanied by adherence to traditional regulatory requirements and NRC oversight as a way to build public confidence in the commercial deployment of this technology.

Looking even longer-term, an aggressive government-industry nuclear RD&D program can help form the basis for advanced (Generation IV) nuclear reactor and fuel cycle technologies that may be deployed around the middle of the century. Today, the U.S. DOE's Advanced Reactor Concepts program is supporting R&D on advanced reactor concepts, including liquid metal-cooled fast reactors and liquid fluoride salt-cooled reactors; in addition, DOE is supporting the development of technologies (such as a supercritical CO_2 Brayton cycle for energy conversion) that could be applied to many different reactor technologies.[127] The United States should continue to invest in these types of long-term R&D efforts, including investments in the university- and national laboratory-based research infrastructure needed to develop and demonstrate new nuclear technologies.

EXPANDED PARTICIPATION IN INTERNATIONAL NUCLEAR COOPERATION

According to the Blue Ribbon Commission on America's Nuclear Future: "Safety is an inescapable, continuing, expensive, and technologically sophisticated demand that all new entrants to commercial nuclear power will have to confront over the full lifecycle of these systems—from preparing for construction through decommissioning. The nature and scope of the safety challenges involved might not be fully apparent to new entrants. Managing these challenges requires that robust institutional, organizational and technical arrangements be in place at the very early stages of a nuclear program. Also needed are sufficient technical knowledge and experience, strong management, continued peer-review and training, and an enduring commitment to excellence and a robust safety culture."[128]

The United States is widely respected internationally for its strong independent nuclear regulator and its successful industry self-governance model. The accident at the Fukushima-Daiichi nuclear

---

[126] Richard B. Andres and Hanna L. Breetz, "Small Nuclear Reactors for Military Installations: Capabilities, Costs, and Technological Implications," Strategic Forum, National Defense University, February 2011, http://www.ndu.edu/inss/docuploaded/SF%20262%20Andres.pdf.

[127] U.S. Department of Energy, "FY 2013 Congressional Budget Request," Volume 3, p. 313.

[128] Blue Ribbon Commission on America's Nuclear Future (BRC), Final Report to the Secretary of Energy, January 2012, p. 110.

plant in Japan reinforces the need for the United States to encourage expanded international efforts to promote the safe operation of existing and planned nuclear installations.

As other countries pursue ambitious programs of nuclear investment, the United States can fill an important role by helping them tackle the safe planning, design, construction, operation, and regulation of nuclear energy systems. A strengthened U.S. nuclear industry will help preserve this opportunity and will ensure that developing nuclear nations look first to the United States as a source of nuclear know-how.

As we noted in previous chapters, the NRC is regularly engaged as the benchmark standard setter for regulators in other countries and the Institute of Nuclear Power Operations (INPO) is routinely approached for leadership and assistance in applying the same principles that govern U.S. industry nuclear operations to other operators around the globe. The World Association of Nuclear Operators (WANO), modeled after INPO, is evolving to influence safe operations on a global basis. More recently, the International Framework for Nuclear Energy Cooperation (IFNEC) has evolved as an influential forum, with 62 participating nations, and a five-nation steering committee (United States, United Kingdom, France, Japan, and China); it has been embraced by many countries expanding or seeking to enter the realm of nuclear operations as a key opportunity for gaining insight from the experiences of successful nuclear energy nations. With continued DOE leadership, IFNEC, in particular, offers a promising venue for bringing forward and reinforcing standards and principles for responsible and safe nuclear energy operations worldwide. Through these entities and others, the United States should continue to leverage its regulatory and legal framework and its reputation for excellence, especially in working with emerging nations that are seeking to establish nuclear energy as a new domestic source of electricity.

SOLVING THE NUCLEAR WASTE CHALLENGE

The January 2012 report of the Blue Ribbon Commission on America's Nuclear Future found that "America's nuclear waste management policy has been troubled for decades and is now all but completely broken down."[129] The U.S. nuclear waste management plan was laid out in the 1980s under the Nuclear Waste Policy Act. In 1987, Yucca Mountain in Nevada was selected as the only site to be evaluated for an underground repository for high-level nuclear waste. If the site was found to be suitable, it was to begin receiving waste in 1998. Yet, despite more than 20 years of work and more than $10 billion spent, the Yucca Mountain repository has not been constructed and has been proposed for termination.

Currently, more than 65 thousand metric tons of spent commercial reactor fuel are being stored at about 75 sites around the country. Each year, the operation of commercial nuclear reactors in the United States generates another 2,000 to 2,400 metric tons of spent fuel. DOE is also storing thousands of tons of spent fuel and high-level radioactive waste from defense and research programs at government-owned sites.[130]

Demonstrating a credible path forward for nuclear waste management in the United States would both reduce public concerns about nuclear plant construction and satisfy laws in several states

---

[129] Blue Ribbon Commission on America's Nuclear Future (BRC), Final Report to the Secretary of Energy, January 2012, p. 110, p. iii.
[130] Blue Ribbon Commission on America's Nuclear Future (BRC), Final Report to the Secretary of Energy, January 2012, pp. 14–19.

that prohibit new plant construction without a solution to the nuclear waste problem. The dual challenges of spent nuclear fuel management and disposal are addressed at length in the final 2012 report of the Blue Ribbon Commission on America's Nuclear Future and the 2011 MIT Report on the Future of the Nuclear Fuel Cycle.[131] We urge that the U.S. government act on the recommendations in these reports as a critical step toward supporting the revival of the nuclear industry in the United States, including:

- Providing access to the funds nuclear utility ratepayers provide for the purpose of nuclear waste management.
- Establishing a new organization dedicated solely to implementing the waste management program and empowered with the authority and resources to succeed.
- Implementing a consent-based approach to siting future nuclear waste management facilities.
- Pursuing fuel-leasing options for countries that have or are pursuing small nuclear programs. These options should provide incentives to forego uranium enrichment and should incorporate spent-fuel take-back arrangements.
- Undertaking integrated system studies and experiments on innovative reactor and fuel cycle options, and selecting a limited set of options for more detailed analysis.

Industry groups and waste management experts have concluded that implementation of these recommendations is essential to getting the U.S. nuclear waste program back on track and thereby eliminating one of the major obstacles to restoring the U.S. nuclear energy enterprise.[132] As the Blue Ribbon Commission stated: "First, with so many players in the international nuclear technology and policy arena, the United States will increasingly have to lead by engagement and by example. Second, the United States cannot exercise effective leadership on issues related to the back end of the nuclear fuel cycle so long as its own program is in disarray; effective domestic policies are needed to support America's international agenda."[133]

The United States can regain some of its lost influence by working with its allies to offer other countries—especially countries with relatively new or small nuclear programs—upstream and downstream fuel cycle services (i.e., beyond just reactor design, construction, and operation). Such services could be extremely valuable for limiting proliferation risks and ensuring that global nuclear energy development proceeds in a way that protects all countries' safety and security interests. Specifically, the ability to offer not only uranium enrichment services but also spent-fuel takeback and disposal or reprocessing at facilities under rigorous multinational security safeguards and controls could be extremely valuable.

ECONOMIC SUPPORT AND FINANCIAL STRUCTURING FOR NEW U.S. REACTORS

A limited set of "first mover" financial incentives at both the federal and state levels can help jump-start the construction of new nuclear power plants in the United States. Below we present a wide array of options and opportunities for encouraging and facilitating investment in new construction. We recognize that the approaches presented below would all be costly and would be

---

[131] Several members of this Commission served on or otherwise contributed to the work of the Blue Ribbon Commission and the MIT study group.

[132] For example, see Nuclear Energy Institute, Press Release, "Nuclear Energy Stakeholders Welcome Blue Ribbon Commission Report to DOE," January 26, 2012, http://www.nei.org/newsandevents/newsreleases/nuclear-energy-stakeholders-welcome-blue-ribbon-commission-report-to-doe.

[133] Blue Ribbon Commission on America's Nuclear Future (BRC), Report to the Secretary of Energy, January 2012, p. xiv.

quite challenging to enact in this time of tight government budgets. We offer a range of options, not with the expectation that all of them will be adopted, but with the conviction that implementing any of these options—at the federal level, within individual states, or both—will improve prospects for building several more new plants in the United States and thus help strengthen the U.S. nuclear industry.

When considering how to advance the construction of new nuclear reactors in the United States, it is useful to consider actions that can be taken in the three major phases of nuclear plant construction: design, build, and operate.

- The "design" phase includes all the steps involved in getting a reactor site and reactor design licensed for construction. This phase can be as short as two to three years initially, assuming a standardized version of the design has already been approved by the NRC, and can be even shorter for the fourth or fifth unit constructed at a given site.
- The "build" phase includes all phases of engineering, procurement, and construction, including the startup testing that will be required before the plant can enter commercial service. For purposes of this discussion, we assume the build phase lasts six years.
- The "operations" phase represents those activities after the plant enters commercial operation.

Using our Design/Build/Operate (DBO) model, we illustrate the revenues and expenses for each phase. We assume the design phase lasts two years followed by a six-year build phase. The plant is then assumed to operate for 40 years. While a longer operating life is certainly possible and may be an important factor in considering new plant proposals from the perspective of a generator or a public utility commission, whether a plant operates longer than 40 years is fairly irrelevant to the financial analysis given the long period of discounting that applies.

Critical to finding willing investors for the build phase will be the presence of policies that support the private sector's economic considerations and risk management objectives. While current U.S. nuclear companies may not choose to be part of a build investor consortium, it is possible that several large companies, heretofore not directly involved, could be interested. Such companies would be ones that value the tax credits, can take a long-term view of the economics, and are large enough not to be financially strained by the size of investments required, even when considering multiple projects (5+) over a period of 10–15 years. These could include:

- Large global energy resource companies
- Large global industrial companies
- Large and long-term investors (such as pension funds)
- Investment arms or companies of the largest countries that have a strategic interest in advancing nuclear energy (e.g., China, Russia, France, South Korea)

LOWER THE COST OF BORROWING

On $7 billion of debt, a 1 percent decrease in the interest rate saves $45 million per year after tax in the early years. This reduction in borrowing costs could be achieved in at least two ways:

- Federal loan guarantees—As discussed elsewhere in this report, the DOE loan guarantee program established by the Energy Policy Act of 2005 has been implemented in a manner that is inconsistent with the intent of the program and that has not proved successful in spurring investment in new nuclear construction in the United States. It should be reviewed and revised in order to provide support for new light-water reactor (LWR) construction and SMR development.

- Relaxed restrictions on foreign investment—Encouraging broad opportunities for foreign ownership in new nuclear construction would ease the investment burden on relatively small market cap firms in the United States. This will require changes to relevant codes and regulations so that sovereign wealth funds, foreign investors, non-U.S.-owned companies, and pension funds are free to invest in U.S. nuclear plants. Foreign ownership should be allowed up to 90 percent of the equity value of the facility, contingent on the requirement that a U.S.-based owner/operator recognized by the NRC retains a controlling interest. All matters related to the safety, security, and reliability of the facility, including the unalterable right to make capital calls on the owners of the facility in support of the safety, security, and reliability needs of the facility, would remain with the U.S. owner/operator.
- The possibility of engaging the investment arms of nations that are making strategic investments in nuclear energy is complicated by rules that restrict foreign interests in U.S. nuclear power plants. Foreign ownership, control, and influence of U.S. nuclear facilities is governed by sections 103d and 104d of the Atomic Energy Act of 1954. Legal writings on this issue have found that "The statutory and regulatory restrictions on foreign ownership, control, and domination should not be read to preclude foreign investment in a nuclear facility, so long as the AEA licensee is a U.S. corporation (or other U.S. entity), provided the licensee is not directly and wholly owned by a foreign corporation or other foreign entity, and U.S. citizens control any decisions on matters affecting the common defense and security, such as the control of special nuclear material. This means, for example, that a licensee under sections 103 or 104 of the AEA could be a wholly owned, indirect subsidiary of a foreign corporation (the foreign corporation could be the 'grandparent' of the NRC licensee), provided that U.S. citizens control any decisions affecting the common defense and security."[134]

REVISIONS TO THE TAX CODE

The federal tax code provides mechanisms for the federal government to incentivize activities that are in the national interest and that the marketplace would not otherwise undertake. The Energy Policy Act of 2005 moved in this direction. Given the experience of the last several years, and the increased gap in the economic viability of new nuclear facilities, further expansion of these mechanisms would be beneficial in the following areas.

- Accelerated depreciation (also known as "bonus depreciation") involves changes to relevant tax codes to provide for depreciation at the time that investments are made. This kind of incentive provides benefits during the construction period, effectively offsetting the capital requirements for a new plant as it is being constructed. One must assume the tax depreciation benefit can be used by a parent company or investors with offsetting earnings. The result is shown as a reduction to debt and/or equity required to build the plant. This method does not require outlays from the government—simply a change in when the tax benefit of depreciation is realized.
- One option that should be considered for new nuclear plants is a 30 percent investment tax credit (ITC) upon project completion. The ITC serves to reduce the net investment in

---

[134] Martin G. Malsch, "The Purchase of U.S. Nuclear Power Plants by Foreign Entities," *Energy Law Journal*, Vol. 20:263, http://felj.org/elj/Energy%20Journals/Vol20_No2_1999_Art_Purchase%20of%20U.S.%20Nuc.pdf.

the plant and associated tax depreciation. Thus, the net benefit of the depreciation benefit (applied to a 35 percent tax rate) and the ITC benefit (30 percent tax credit) is not an additive 65 percent reduction in the overall capital requirement (35 percent tax rate + 30 percent ITC), but rather amounts to a 54.5 percent benefit (30 percent ITC + 35 percent on the remaining 70 percent). An ITC might be necessary for only a limited time, as efficiencies gained through experience with the first few plants could make up the difference after that.

- Property tax abatement encourages state and local authorities to support an approach that excludes new facilities from property taxes for the first 10 years of operation, with a phase-in of low tax requirements for the subsequent 5 years. This would allow the expected increase in power prices due to inflation to potentially cover anticipated property tax expenses.

MONETIZATION OF EXTERNAL BENEFITS

Mechanisms to provide monetary recognition of the societal benefits of certain forms of energy supply (such as low emissions and electricity supply diversification) would improve the prospects for new nuclear builds. Such mechanisms would have the effect of increasing the cost-competitiveness of nuclear-generated electricity. Given uncertainty regarding legislation to regulate carbon emissions, a more realistic means of monetizing the external benefits of nuclear-generated electricity may be through power purchase agreements with the U.S. government, including military bases.

These purchases could offer government entities price stability over a long contract period (possibly 20 years or more). Price assurances could be combined with efforts to permit and

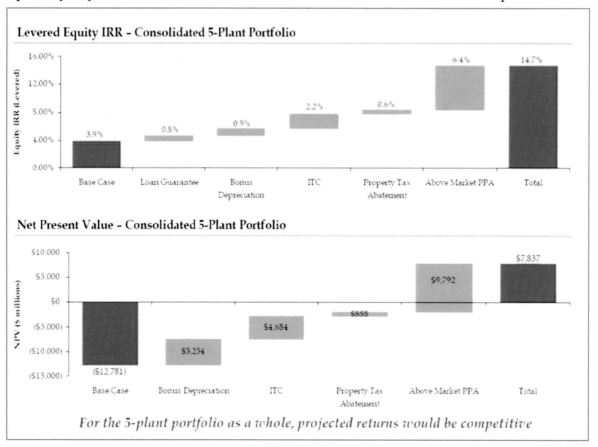

For the 5-plant portfolio as a whole, projected returns would be competitive

encourage the development of a nuclear energy facility on or adjacent to a military facility, with provisions for direct support from the military facility (such as land use easements and facility security) included as part of the project.

Combining these options and applying them to the basic financial model presented in Chapter 3, the property tax, accelerated depreciation, ITC, power price, and loan guarantee/financing provisions would result in a positive return on equity for a first nuclear reactor project. Looking at the complete program of five new reactors used in this analysis, the levered equity internal rate of return (IRR) would increase from 3.9 percent to 14.7 percent. The net present value (NPV) of the five-plant portfolio would increase from -$12.78 billion to +$7.84 billion (see the figure above).

The set of policy options discussed above is, of course, not exhaustive. Policymakers who are interested in creating the conditions under which the U.S. nuclear enterprise can be restored will want to consider these and other options as they craft supportive policies.

Scenario	Description	Plant #1 Cost ($ bn)	Plant #5 Cost ($ bn)	Consolidated Portfolio Cost ($ bn)
A	Loan Guarantee [1]	$0.3	$0.2	$1.1
B	Bonus Depreciation	$1.4	$0.8	$5.2
C	Investment Tax Credit	$1.2	$0.7	$4.7
D	Property Tax Abatement	$0.2	$0.1	$0.9
E	Long-Term PPA	$2.2	$1.7	$9.8
	Total	$5.3	$3.5	$21.7

Of course, all of these incentives would come at a cost. The increase in NPV to the plant effectively represents the value transfer from the entity offering the enhancement. This value transfer could amount, on average, to approximately $4.4 billion per plant or up to $21.7 billion for the entire five-plant portfolio.

INTERNAL GOVERNMENT POLICY COORDINATION

Successful implementation of the above recommendations could be better assured if it is backed by senior-level policy coordination within the U.S. government. Such coordination could take many forms and we don't presume to know what arrangements will work best within a given administration or congressional body. Options include but are not limited to:

- A White House-directed activity, providing interagency coordination;
- A Cabinet member assigned responsibility for interagency coordination; and
- Congressional oversight of federal activities, either through a specific mandate to an existing committee(s) or through the establishment of a new oversight entity.

Consideration should also be given to forming a private-sector stakeholder advisory committee with representation from nuclear plant owners and operators, investors, labor groups, nuclear vendors and contractors, the financial sector, state officials, environmental advocates, and other organizations. This group would provide critical expertise and insight from outside the federal government in support of ongoing efforts to maintain nuclear energy as a key component of electricity generation in the United States.

DEVELOPING THE FUTURE NUCLEAR WORKFORCE

As discussed in Chapter 3, new nuclear energy facilities will fuel demand for a whole new generation of skilled nuclear professionals. From design engineers to construction specialists to operating and maintenance staff, a new wave of nuclear plants will create a need for tens to hundreds of thousands of trained nuclear workers. To be fully prepared to design and construct new nuclear facilities, the nuclear energy industry and the U.S. government will need to invest heavily in education, training, and workforce development.

Some of this investment is already taking place to help maintain indispensable skills for the sector. Nuclear-related programs at universities receive annual federal funding in the form of scholarships and grants. With this assistance, students are able to pursue research that is crucial to developing advanced nuclear technologies. Most of this assistance is distributed by the Department of Energy, the National Nuclear Security Administration, and the Nuclear Regulatory Commission, but other agencies, such as the Department of Labor and the National Science Foundation, also play an important role. We clearly support continuation of these programs, given their importance in helping preserve domestic capacity.

Appendix: Key Contributors to the CSIS Nuclear Energy Program

Principal Authors and Editors

- Michael Wallace, CSIS U.S. Nuclear Energy Project
- John Kotek, Consultant
- Sarah Williams, CSIS U.S. Nuclear Energy Project
- Paul Nadeau, CSIS
- Thomas Hundertmark, McKinsey & Company
- George David Banks, CSIS

Financial Structuring Subgroup

- David Anderson, Consultant
- John Collins, Consultant
- Paul Dabbar, JP Morgan
- Henry Decker, Moelis and Co.
- Andrew Good, Constellation Energy
- David Hill, Sidley Austin LLP
- Jeffrey Holzschuh, Morgan Stanley
- Richard Myers, Nuclear Energy Institute
- Simon Pratt, Rothschild, Inc.
- Darryl Sagel, Rothschild, Inc.
- Roger Wood, Moelis & Company

External Experts

- Jim Asseltine, Barclays Capital
- Carol Berrigan, Nuclear Energy Institute
- Gerry Cauley, North American Electric Reliability Corporation
- Francisco de la Chesnaye, Electric Power Research Institute
- Jim Connaughton, Constellation Energy
- Joyce Connery, National Security Council
- Admiral John Grossenbacher (Ret.), Idaho National Laboratory
- Craig Hanson, Babcock & Wilcox Nuclear Energy
- Jeffrey Holzschuh, Morgan Stanley
- Chairman Gregory Jaczko, former chairman, Nuclear Regulatory Commission
- Revis James, Electric Power Research Institute
- John Kotek, Consultant
- Dr. Peter Lyons, U.S. Department of Energy
- Dr. Howard McFarlane, Idaho National Laboratory
- Larry Makovich, IHS CERA
- Edward McGinnis, U.S. Department of Energy
- Richard Myers, Nuclear Energy Institute
- Daniel Poneman, U.S. Department of Energy

- Jonathan Silver, U.S. Department of Energy

- Roger Wood, Moelis & Company

Additional CSIS contributors:
- Craig Cohen, CSIS Executive Vice President
- Jane Nakano, CSIS Energy and National Security Program
- David Pumphrey, CSIS Energy and National Security Program
- Bradford Simmons, CSIS U.S. Nuclear Energy Program

Donors:
- American Electric Power
- Areva
- Babcock & Wilcox Nuclear Energy
- Constellation Energy
- Duke Energy
- Exelon
- GE Hitachi
- MidAmerican Energy Company
- Mitsubishi Nuclear
- Nuclear Energy Institute
- Sargent & Lundy
- Urenco
- United Association of Plumbers and Pipefitters of the United States and Canada
- Westinghouse

A special thanks to the many additional people that attended our forums and provided important input to the process along the way.